GREAT WRITERS GREAT STORIES

edited by

Edward Allan Faine

IM Press

First Printing 1999

Manufactured in the United States of America

IM Press
P.O. Box 5346
Takoma Park, Maryland 20913-5346
301-587-1202

Autographed copies of this book can be ordered through **IM Press** at the above address. Send a $15 check (includes postage and handling) for each copy **ordered**. (See back page 224 for additional ordering information)

Library of Congress Catalog Card Number: 98-75536

ISBN 0-9654651-6-0

Cover and back photos
(Spring scenes at the United States
National Arboretum)
by Gerald A. Consalvi

And in case you're wondering, the flowering shrubs on the back cover are *Astilbe* (False Spirea).

Who with reason despises the day of small things.

Zachariah 4: 10

NOTE TO READERS

Great writing, great story-telling is alive and well in the mid-Atlantic.

This book—a celebratory showcase for twenty-seven great story tellers—is proof positive. Twelve of these writers have broken through the paper ceiling and have published a book or two, and seventeen have received major literary awards. All have celebrity potential.

These great writers share two things in common. They reside in Maryland, Virginia, or Washington, D.C.; and their stories—included herein—were first published in the literary magazine FODDERWING (point your browzer to www.magamall.com, and select literary). Otherwise, their writing styles and subject matter are as diverse as the population and geography of the three aforementioned states.

If you agree with me that these are indeed great stories, register your comment on the amazon.com site for this book. Your endorsement will bring this book to the attention of other discriminating readers and the "New York book scouts." Then we can all laze back and watch the searing heat of celebrity sunshine burn off the fog of anonymity and expose these emerging writers—and their work—to a wider audience.

Edward Allan Faine
Editor
June, 1999

CONTENTS

CONTENTS

IT COULD BE WORSE

by

R. R. Angell

You are mashing your naked, chapped lips together while standing in front of the elevators at your god-forsaken job, fingering the lipstick in your pocket that you wished you had put on in the car, and now have to wait until you get to the ladies lounge. The carpal tunnel in your left hand is already starting to throb at the thought of pounding the keyboard for yet another day of coding for the-man-upstairs. The doctor told you to wear your wrist brace, avoid salt and caffeine, and please try to de-stress. De-stress hell.

You're late because you can't get going because you can't drink your coffee because of the stupid ulcer because of the god-forsaken job and now you have a headache and you ran out of Zantac yesterday and you pretty much feel like no one gives a shit so why should you. You smooth the now blonde hair you spent all last night dyeing and think about how long it will take to get split ends as you look at yourself in the mirrored elevator door.

You rub your nose and wipe your hand across your dry lips without thinking, trying to let your mind go blank. Maybe it's possible to achieve some sort of Zen meditative state, where you can sleepwalk through work and come alive when they hand you the paycheck on your way out the door Friday night; to consciously live your nights and unconsciously dredge for the money during the day. You feel your stomach twinge and your spirit drop as you think about your nights, lonely and boring as they are, and consider that your life is pretty much a slightly overweight black-and-white photograph of no consequence, no color except for your golden retriever, Boris, that your hair now matches. People always look like their dogs. Maybe this is the first step. Great.

The elevator next to yours is the one that opens, and you push in front of this geeky guy with slick black hair, thick rimmed glasses, wearing a tan trench coat, and you think, *is he smelling my hair?* You look at him in the reflecting finish of the doors on the way up, and he has his eyes closed with this look of ecstasy on his face, and you wonder if he is masturbating or something, and you smile just as he opens his eyes and looks directly into yours and smiles back. *Oh god. How gross. Who is this loser anyway? Wait until Marge hears about this.*

Fortunately, the doors open before you laugh out loud, and you escape into a carpeted waiting room populated with expensive rattan furniture and those little office trees. It's not your floor, but you had to get out of there. A guy in a blue pinstripe suite gets off just behind you, making a big deal about stepping around you on his way toward the receptionist who greets him with "good morning Dr. Blancher," and a sickly sweet smile before leveling her eyes on you.

You see *Highlights* magazines on the coffee table and you know you are in a dentist's office. The sound of a drill gnaws at your ears, and someone else clears his throat behind you. The receptionist is still staring. You are obviously in the wrong place.

Someone says, "Excuse me, I..., I ..." in a wimpy little voice to your right, and you turn and find the jack-off standing there and you laugh out loud into his face. You can't help it so you cover your mouth.

"Oh my gosh. I'm on the wrong floor," you say to him as you punch the button and hope another elevator is only seconds away.

"Me, uh. Me too," he says looking around a little lost. "Um, um, I work upstairs. At Daimes Engineering. I'm an engineer."

And I'm not, geek, so blow. But instead you say, "That's nice," and let the silence between you highlight the metal scream of the drill. He shoves a hand into his pocket and he fishes around in there, and you glance toward the receptionist, hoping she is taking this all in. You start to wonder if maybe she has a gun and can shoot him.

"Um, here is my card." He retrieves a business card out of *that* pocket, and hands it to you. You are afraid to take it, having this sudden image of it being warm and moist and untouchable. You look at it cooling between his delicate fingers, yes delicate, probably from never doing any manual labor and all that hand cream he uses to.... You take a deep breath.

To your surprise, you actually take the card and wonder why you are doing this against your will. It says: Elmond C. Verdmung, Professional Engineer.

"Interesting name."

"It was my mother's," he says, and you wonder what kind of idiot he is, named after his mother, "um, her father's name really. Family name. Can I take you to lunch?"

You realize that he has been falling all over himself because of you, and he jumped off the elevator because of some infatuation-thing. You look into the mirrored doors and make a note to keep your hair that color, and the elevator light goes out so you blurt, "I'm not sure, it's too early."

"What's your name?"

"Selma. Selma Blought." You forgot to leave off your last name. Or lie. Your heart is fluttering. You're flattered, and then startled as the elevator doors open and you both press inside together.

"Please call me," he says as you get off. "Please." You look back over your shoulder as the doors close and see him give a gentle wave with his fingertips. Christ.

You drag Marge into the lounge right away and tell her. She primps your hair and coos at you, wrinkling her big Bette Midler nose in your face.

"Geeks make great providers, Selma. I married one, and you've seen our house. Not bad in bed either. A little quick at first, but you know, they don't mess around on you. They're as loyal as puppies." She looks around the empty ladies lounge and whispers, "I'm going to quit this place as soon as I can get pregnant." She taps her forehead with her finger.

"Should I go to lunch with him, just like that?" You really feel out on a limb on this one, and are ready for someone to shove you in the right direction.

"Why not? Go to a public place and get a free lunch. What can go wrong? You can always leave." She has a point. "But, honey, don't phone him."

He can't phone me, he doesn't have my number."

"Oh, Selma." You resent her looking at you that way,

as if you were stupid and only she can help you. "Email him!" She pats you on the sleeve. "Tell him you'll go by email! It's the surest way to a geek's heart."

"You think?" You look at her coyly and bat your eyes, warming up.

"I know it! Now meet me back here on your break and we'll *make* you up *to kill.* Oh, how romantic! Who would have thought!" Marge breezes out, leaving you with the mirror. What did she mean 'who would have thought?'

You shrug it off and email him. He emails you back almost instantly. *It* is on.

The girls in the office know already, and they all want to know where you're having lunch. You just say that you are meeting him down in the lobby by the revolving door. They chatter about going with you to see what he's like. No way. He's yours until you dump him. Maybe he *is* the one. Maybe you *could* use another puppy. Boris wouldn't mind. After all, a man is a different species.

Lunch was pleasant. Elmond is sweet. What a surprise. He was even quiet.

"That tells you. Some privacy in the relationship is a good thing," Marge says as she reaches in to adjust your dress. The black hairs on her arms seem thicker today, and she has more little moles under that canopy of hair than you remember.

That night he calls you at 9:30. Dinner tomorrow? Your heart does a little flutter dance. Someone wants you, and you take a breath and bask in the radiance. Boris looks up from his water bowl, foam dripping from his lips.

"Sure, I would like that. Indian is fine," you say, and you remember this great all-you-can-eat buffet place and you salivate like Pavlov, then think about what chowing down on a first date would look like, and you check yourself. "Chinese would be good too, there's this new fusion place not far from here." You want to go there since it's expensive and trendy, and you hear they have good Mai Tai's. You hesitantly give him your correct address on Battery Place, just off Beall street. He'll call from his car phone.

"Car Phone!" the girls at work squeal and suggest first time perfumes. Cecilia asks with big red painted lips if you are going to wear white at your wedding, and you smile, and in your best Scarlet O'Hara you spit back, "Why yes, I don't know nuthin' 'bout 'bortin' no babies, honey." Cecilia flushes bright orange at the insinuation and stamps out to answer the phone.

He has a Chevy Nova. An old Chevy Nova, with chipping blue paint and a crinkle in the door where it was blown open once by a gust of wind. You flop in the front seat, disappointed since you expected a black BMW, not a cracked vinyl dashboard. He has a nice portable phone that he takes inside the restaurant with him, saying that someone at work might need to ask him a question. You think this is a little overdone, then are totally embarrassed when the phone rings during drinks, at exactly eight fifteen. Weird, since you are looking at the body-builder bartender and the neon clock is directly above his biceps. Everyone turns to stare at your table including the bartender, who shakes his head and looks away.

Prince-Elmond-C-Verdmung-Charming really isn't. It hits you like Boris' tongue, so you order the biggest dish on the menu to go with that bottle of wine you intend to chug, and follow it with the most expensive dessert on the menu. You feel great. To hell with the office witches. He will think you're a porker in no time and run for the hills, but you see admiration in his eyes. No, it's adoration, and you think, oh my God.

He drops you off and leans close; his breath tainted by the green flecks rotting between his teeth. He kisses you on the cheek, missing your lips as you turn your head. You feel trampled by his affections and send him scurrying back to his nasty little engineer's car. So you climb up the stairs to the garage apartment you rent from Mrs. Blakenschtoop, the nosey widow who sometimes lets herself in to deliver the mail just so she can snoop around. At least she loves dogs.

Elmonday calls to let you know he got home safely. "Too bad," you say, then "I can't see you anymore, Elmaroon. Sorry." You hang up.

You remember to thank Endora from all those reruns of *Bewitched* for teaching you how to destroy a name properly. The next thing you know the alarm clock is ringing and Boris is whining to go out. Your head has seen better days so you snooze a few times.

Marge lands on you like a deerfly as soon as you step into the office. Halfway through telling her that Mr. Elmo C. Bird-dung was a ditzy nerd and you ate him into bankruptcy, Cecilia and Toni interrupt and make you start all over again as they ply you with a fresh cup of coffee. The aspirin and attention is kicking in and you are feeling much better. You embellish a little, and tell them that you don't want to deal with this guy's self-esteem problems. Anyone else is welcome to him as far as you're concerned.

That night, Emron still doesn't get it when he calls. You try to go easy on him at first, tell him that he is too good for you, that he deserves better. He wants to read you a bedtime poem. You hang-up. Then you move the Caller ID box into the bedroom and plug it in so you can ignore him from now on. You feel anxious and realize it is that time of month. You take a deep breath and resolve to take it easy.

Boris throws up on his morning walk. You consider giving him a Zantac and wonder what he ate while you weren't looking. You will have to watch him over the next few days to see what happens, but right now you have to get to work, and he should be okay.

No emails from Eldung got through the twit filter. It's going to take a lot to make you smile today besides Midol. Marge quietly shares your coffee breaks. She's a good friend. At least it's Friday night, and you can stay in bed all weekend if you want.

A note on your door from the landlady goes on and on about a nice young man who stopped by, so she put the things inside, hope you don't mind, have a nice weekend, and if you need help with the chocolate to call her.

The smell hits you as soon as you walk through the kitchen door. A vase of roses wrapped in cellophane is lying in a greenish puddle on the counter. There is a shredded two-pound Godiva box on the floor and tooth-marked chocolate fragments dot the tile. The smell is coming from dark splats. Some of the splats have blood in them. You yell for Boris. The smell intensifies in the living room and there are piles of brown goo on the carpet and you fight back a gagging feeling.

Boris is lying in the bathroom. Poop and blood are everywhere. His tail thumps twice and he tries to raise his head from the cold ceramic floor, and you puke into the toilet with the image of pain on his face burned into your mind. You grab two big towels and wrap him up, somehow managing to pick up all eighty-five pounds of him, and get him to the car. You aren't crying; you're driven. The vet lets you stay as she pokes and prods and you finally break down when she shakes her head and leaves you alone with the body. Chocolate induced diarrhea on top of a stomach problem. No charge. Thirty-dollar disposal fee.

Marge picks you up. In her kitchen, she pours a Mai Tai for you and offers you food. You aren't hungry, you just drink. And you cry. And you hug. In the morning, you realize that you have strained your back carrying Boris, and you can barely get up out of their guest bed.

Marge spends Saturday helping you clean up the mess, doing most of the work herself. You straighten up the roses and open the card. It is all from Elmond, the bastard, and you tear into the roses with both frenzied hands ripping them in clumps out of the cellophane. The vase falls to the floor, shattering around your feet. Marge helps pull the thorns out with tweezers and soothing words.

Later the apartment smells like citrus cleanser, and the heat is finally compensating for the open windows, and then the phone rings. You hold up a bandaided hand as Marge reaches to get it. You run into the bedroom and see *his* name on the Caller ID. Marge is behind you. You shake your head and point to the box and whisper "shhh" as if he could hear you, and then you shake uncontrollably as Marge holds you. You check the display and see that he has called throughout the night and almost every hour all morning. The answering machine is full. Your back spasms and you know you have to see a doctor. Marge touches your shoulder and you jump with nerves, throwing the spasms into painful overdrive. Her cousin's a lawyer, but you ask if she knows a hit man first, and the thought makes you feel just a little better.

§ § §

Robert Angell *of Bethesda, Maryland is a recipient of the Jenny McKean Moore award for fiction (1996), Severn School Creative Writing Award (1975), and was recently awarded a residency fellowship at Virginia Center for the Creative Arts. Angell has finished two high-tech thrillers and is working on a collection of short stories and his third novel, this time a literary one. "The work that has been getting the most attention so far is on the literary side, so this next novel is a logical development." Angell's first novel has been nominated for a Pushcart Press Editors' Book Award and the screenplay adaptation was a 1997 Chesterfield Film Competition Semifinalist. His short fiction has appeared in* The Baltimore Review, *and* Gargoyle.

CLICK

by

Jodi Bloom

How David came to be involved with a herd of fat grazing beef cows that lived in his suburban neighborhood was this. One lazy afternoon the previous summer, he was hanging around his neighbor Rachel's house before she had to go to work, and she showed him the grainy black and white photographs she'd taken of them, cows in groups of three or five, sometimes a solo portrait. In the pictures, which she'd printed in the darkroom at her college up north, the cows stood staring straight at you with their big wet eyes and it was weird—the dumb animals actually looked beautiful, silent and majestic. *The majestic cows*, David had called them and Rachel laughed.

"They're just cows," she'd said, "but it's a kick-ass name for a rock band." Rachel laughed again and David felt proud. "You're so bloody British, little rich boy," she teased, giving him a shove. The way she said it David thought it was a compliment, at least sort of.

"Not British, Rach," he'd corrected her, exaggerating his accent for effect. "Afrikaner."

He didn't correct her about the rich boy thing. His mother, Irene, had everyone on the cul-de-sac convinced they were still loaded, filthy rich, like they had been before fleeing Johannesburg and arriving in south Florida, with nothing but the clothes in their suitcases and a line of credit. David didn't want to confuse things or try to explain about rich white people bailing out of South Africa. He didn't really understand the situation himself, anyway.

Along with the cow photos, Rachel also had some sexy nude portraits of her college roommate, a girl who was skinny like a fashion model, with tiny breasts and endless legs, posing in front of what appeared to be an abandoned building. *It was an assignment, you pervert*, Rachel said when David smiled and raised his eyebrows at her. *Studies of the human form*, she added, *so don't get any twisted ideas.* Too late, David thought. He had already pictured Rach and the roommate naked and going at it in their dorm. But he kept quiet.

That was last summer. This summer, although Rachel wasn't home from college yet, highschool had let out and David had his project planned. Photography had infected him, or maybe it was just Rachel. She'd said photography was the perfect medium, the head-on collision of art and science. *Like making something beautiful while you play with your chemistry set*, she had explained, measuring the acrid white powders into tall clear plastic beakers, stirring and watching the temperatures carefully.

And to find truth you must respect the integrity of your subject, Rachel said, quoting one of her professors. David had been thinking of the Crystal Light instant lemonade his mother was addicted to, as he watched the chemical powder swirl in the beaker. That, and Rachel's plump round tits, which were clearly visible, nipples and all, through her white t-shirt. *Truth*? What was she talking about? Besides, how in the world could you respect a herd of ignorant cows—so stupid they stood around waiting to die, so fearful, you could only take one picture at a time of them. Well, whatever. Seeing as there was nothing much else on his summer schedule, and studies of the human form were basically and unfortunately out of the question, David was willing to give the cows a try.

Rachel had explained the procedure of photographing cows one day at the field. First, you tip-toed up to the fence and you had to be dead quiet. Then you waited. Then you waited some more in absolute silence. Eventually, you would see the herd inch toward you from their position way out in the pasture. They came so slow you could barely tell they were alive at all, and you just had to trust it—they were moving—they always did.

And then suddenly there they would be, standing silent like breathing statues, staring at you eye to eye, right into your viewfinder, as though they *wanted* their pictures taken.

Point, focus, click.

And that was it. Because the click of your shutter would scare those cows right out of their pea-brained minds, and the big lumbering creatures would scatter with a velocity you wouldn't imagine they could muster. "Zero to sixty in eight seconds," David said, smiling.

"Yeah, those are some slow-moving machines," Rachel said, "but boy can they haul ass when they want to."

David figured that if he took one shot per day of the cows he might get two-and-a-half rolls of 36-frame black and white Tri-x film exposed before school started in the fall. That was his basic scheme for the summer, that and hanging out with Rach. And maybe, somehow, declaring his love. Or at least making a move on her.

So every day, David walked up the road, with his father's old Leica hanging heavy around his neck, to snap a picture of the cows. And every day a white Lincoln Town Car cruised by slow and long, the driver watching him as it passed. It was pretty weird, but nothing ever happened, so David didn't mind.

In fact, the first time the white Lincoln followed him up the road toward the cow pasture, David smiled and waved, thinking maybe it was his mother, Irene, playing spy or something from behind the tinted windows of the big car—exactly the same as the one she drove. Tracking him, he'd thought, to see what he was up to, if he was maybe out doing some off-limits activity, like looking for a job.

Aside from his photography project, David was bored to death and a job would have been pretty cool, or at least something to do. Even a job at McDonald's or maybe something up at the Broward Mall—probably all he could get at fifteen—would have been better than hanging around the house all summer waiting for Rachel to come home from college. Besides, he had the feeling his family could use the extra money.

"Absolutely not," David's mom would say, delivering a speech he'd heard too many times. "Things aren't so bad that I will allow my son to participate in child labor ... blah, blah, blah." David's blue eyes (his best feature) would glaze over, and he would think about tying back his wavy light brown hair (second best feature) into one of those ugly burger-boy hairnets. He imagined facing some hot-looking girl that he might like to ask out and having to say: Would you like fries with that? No, maybe things weren't that bad.

Things were bad enough though, that the family would soon be moving a mile up the road—from their lovely but horrifyingly expensive split-level rancher on the Jacaranda golfcourse to a more affordable three-bedroom at the Lehigh apartments—a move that would place David exactly one mile away from Rachel's house, but would also put him exactly one mile closer to the cows. Not exactly an even trade.

David had photographed one other subject in his life besides cows, a shot he was famous for in two places. One night last summer, Rachel had driven them in her father's Buick to a graveyard a few miles outside their neighborhood.

"Follow me," she'd said, getting out of the car. David was falling in love. He had begun to dream of her at night, waking up every morning more horny than usual. *Uh...yeah*, he thought, *right. Follow. No problem.*

For some reason, maybe because of the falling in love, it wasn't at all scary or even weird being there in the graveyard. It was just cool, him and Rachel and the tombstones in the moonlight. He wasn't even thinking about the fact that they were walking on dead people or anything like that.

Rachel climbed up on a huge stone gravemarker in the shape of a cross. She draped herself over it, handing the camera to David. "Here," she commanded, "shoot."

David stepped back and focused. He couldn't believe how incredible she looked, her bare suntanned arms spread out on the huge white marble cross, her head tilted back—a crucifixion, but...sexy-looking. Her gauzy skirt was blowing in the wind, her long brown hair too. It was almost unbearably perfect. He steadied his hands; he didn't want to screw it up.

He checked the f-stop, listened to the flash wind up. Then, just as he clicked the shutter, Rachel did the amazing thing of pulling down the left side of her tube top, exposing one breast, as pale as the marble, with its small, perfectly erect nipple.

"*What is this pornography*?" David's mom exclaimed when she happened upon the print in her son's night table drawer.

"It's *not*..." David said, "it's nothing." He grabbed the picture away from her, careful not to tear it. Then he did stash the photo in the back of his closet with his real porno mags, a fairly decent collection he'd started when he was thirteen. It was a good hiding place.

Besides with David's mother, the second place that "The Crucifixion of Rachel" was famous was at Rachel's college in Maryland, where the photo caused a nudity scandal in a group exhibit at the Undergrad Library.

Rachel called David the night the photo was removed from the show. She railed on the school and the librarian, who she called a crusty old twat. She screamed and yelled about the asshole guys that had been calling her for dates, getting her name off the ID card taped to the wall beneath the print. One guy had even breathed heavily into the phone and asked if she would like him to rape her in a graveyard sometime. Rachel ranted and raved about society, about censorship and sexual repression of women and everything, really—she was so pissed.

"Your name was on the card too," she explained, "so I thought you'd want to know. I doubt you'll get in any trouble though," she added, "I told them you went to another school."

David imagined his name printed on the small white card, below or side-by-side with Rachel's. For some reason, the thought of getting in trouble with Rachel made him incredibly hot.

After the photo incident, David was truly in love. He began waiting immediately for Rachel to come home from college, although it was only January.

Now it was June and he was still waiting. Looking at his camera he saw that he had been waiting exactly 17 days since school had let out. That was the number of pictures he'd taken of the cows, the number of times he'd walked up the hot asphalt road on his assignment—an assignment he fantasized Rachel had given him. And the number of times he had masturbated to the crucifixion picture, which had become his other daily ritual.

Then his family moved up the street to the Lehigh.

The difference was, David's walk to photograph the cows took twelve and a half minutes, instead of the twenty-five it had taken when he lived across the cul-de-sac from Rachel, and, he remembered with longing, could see her bedroom window from his own.

David was thinking about all of this the day that the white Lincoln finally stopped by the side of the road. The dark tinted electric window on the driver's side eased slowly down to reveal not his mother, of course, but a woman about Irene's age—a fairly attractive blonde waving and smiling at him.

"Hi there," she called. She had a red and blue plaid scarf tying back her bouncy blonde hair.

"You live over at the Lehigh don't you?" the woman asked.

"Yep," David said, trying to sound American, just to see how it came out.

"Me too," she said. "5-B."

"Oh," David said. "Right."

"What a cute British accent," the woman said, smiling. "Hey," she added, "you want a ride back? It's hot as Hades out here."

"No, no thanks," David said, "and it's not Brit...oh, never mind," he added, not bothering to explain. Nor did he bother to explain about the cows, about having to get his daily picture of them, which suddenly seemed ridiculous, or immature, or...something.

"Okay," the woman called, "see ya around then?"

"Yeah, sure," David said, turning to continue toward the field.

"I'm Audrey," the woman called as she cruised past. She winked at him. "And you are?"

"David," David said. He flashed a smile at her. What the hell.

It was the twenty-third frame of that first roll of film that Audrey ruined the next time she stopped the Lincoln and blasted her horn at David. In the end he decided it was worth it.

David was standing at the wooden fence, waiting and composing his shot. The herd was approaching, like always, slowly. Rachel said it was sheer torture waiting for the sluggish animals (*majestic, my ass*, she'd say), but David didn't mind. He loved waiting there by the fence, under the big wide Florida sky and the hot tropical sun.

He stood perfectly still; then it happened. The one cow that David had been waiting for the entire summer, the same 23 days he'd been waiting for Rachel, eased herself into his viewfinder—the beautiful pale brown and white who had kept her distance all these weeks. She was a pretty cow, so soft-looking and sweet, and the only one that wasn't your basic black with white splotches. David thought of her as a stunning blonde among a bunch of standard brunettes. He had nicknamed her Debbie Harry, who David thought was (aside from Rachel, of course) the sexiest woman on planet Earth.

But just as Debbie Harry moved into the frame, for a solo portrait no less, Audrey's horn blared and Debbie took off madly across the field with the others.

"Damn it," David said out loud. "Bloody hell."

Then Audrey gave David a ride back to the Lehigh in her Lincoln and fucked him for hours and hours on the big bed in 5-B.

David now had two assignments every day: snap a picture of the cows, and somehow try to please Audrey who was virtually insatiable—the way women were in their thirties, he'd heard. Once more, he thought; one more time and that'll do it. But Audrey never seemed to run out of orgasms, or positions for that matter.

It basically just ended each evening when David had to go home for supper, which he felt was more than slightly embarrassing. Audrey thought it was funny—*tell your mum you won the match*, she'd tease. David had told Irene he was playing tennis with a schoolmate, carrying his racket along as a prop. Then he'd slip down the hallway and make his way around the building to Audrey's place. He never admitted his virginity to her. Besides, with her endless orgasms, he figured he was doing just fine.

David liked Audrey okay. She was a talented dancer, she told him. "Classically fucking trained," she'd said, taking a deep drag on a slender Eve cigaret and blowing smoke rings toward the ceiling. "I just never got my big break." Audrey stretched one plump leg out high above her shoulder, her foot clasped tightly in her hand as she extended. David was mesmerized by her ample naked flesh, her round thighs, the blonde triangle of pubes, her pink snatch with its wet slit—all of it exposed for him to contemplate and touch and do whatever he could think of.

"That's why I'm stuck down at that shit-hole lounge, dancing for a bunch of losers," Audrey said, but David was drawing a line down her outstretched leg with his finger, watching as he slowly slid it in and out of her hole, and he didn't really hear the details of her resumé, or life story, or whatever the fuck she was droning on and on about.

Sometimes Audrey looked pretty weary and worn out. But overall, David liked her okay. He especially liked her big round ass, liked the view of it rising like an enormous pale moon above his cock while he banged into her from behind.

By frame thirty-two (thirty-two cow portraits and an unnamed number of sexual encounters into the summer if you counted each orgasm separately) David wondered whether Rachel was ever coming home. He finally got up the nerve to call her mother.

"Oh *David*," Rachel's mom exclaimed into the phone, "how *are* you? We sure miss your smiling face around here."

We? Did that maybe include Rachel? David felt weird talking to Rachel's mom; he must have been crazy to call. He wondered if a person could tell you were in love from the very sound of your voice.

"Um," he said. "Fine, I'm fine."

"And your mother? How is Irene doing?"

"Fine," David said. "Everyone's just fine."

Silence. David felt extra weird. What if Rachel's mom figured out he was in love with Rachel and told her?

"Uh, is Rach home yet? I mean, is she ... when will Rachel be back from school?" he finally said, trying to act as casual as possible, under the circumstances.

"Oh," Rachel's mom said, "didn't you hear? Rachel got a job. She's staying up north this summer working in the photo-lab at school. She'll be home for Christmas though. Shall I tell her you asked about her?"

"No, that's okay," David said. Then he said goodbye and hung up.

Christmas? It might as well be *forever*. He did the math. Christmas was about one hundred and seventy-five days away. One hundred and seventy-five pictures of a stupid herd of cows. That was a lot of waiting. Bloody fucking hell, David thought. A hundred and seventy-five photographs and probably a thousand and a half fucks with Audrey. A million and a half blow jobs. Billions of ... he rolled over on his bed and fell asleep.

In his dream, David was shooting pictures of Audrey with the Leica. He imitated a fashion photographer he'd seen on TV, moving quick, changing angles—now above his subject, now below. Audrey spread her legs wide and got into some truly fantastic positions, her juicy round butt displayed in full view. Later that week, David was glad he'd had the practice, even if it was only a dream.

"How many god damned boring pictures are you going to take of those cows?" Audrey demanded one bright afternoon in her darkened apartment. David suddenly felt ridiculous, totally fucking ridiculous. It was true, he was bored to death with the big slow-moving beasts; and honestly felt he'd explored the subject to its absolute fucking fullest. Besides, he'd finally gotten his portrait of Debbie Harry twenty frames ago.

"What about little old me?" Audrey had asked, biting her lower lip and eyeing David as though he had hurt her feelings.

David reached for the Leica and ordered her to make love to the camera, just like the guy on TV had said to the model, even though saying the words made him feel like a total jerk. And wouldn't you know it, Audrey, although way more interesting than the suburban cows had been, even at their most fascinating, turned out to be slow-moving too. She'd lounge around on her endless king-sized bed in a tangle of sour sheets, striking lazy sleepy poses. But at least she didn't run off madly after each shot. David's shutter clicked away as Audrey moved closer and closer, until sometimes his viewfinder was filled end to end with just a breast or a curve of her thigh.

§ § §

Jodi Bloom *of Washington, D.C. has been published in numerous literary journals including Gargoyle, Happy, Minimus, The Potomac Review, The Washington Review, and WordWrights. She was recently awarded The Washington Review award for Best Fiction, 1997, and her work appears in the anthologies Fiction 2000 (Red Hen Press), and It's Only Rock and Roll: An Anthology of Rock and Roll Short Stories (Godine, 1998).*

A Toad in the Garden

by

Vonnie Winslow Crist

I kneel on an empty wild bird food bag, begin to weed the sweet-scented woodruff. I've chosen not to wear flowered cotton gloves. Today my palms will be rough and scratched and my fingernails will chip, need to be scrubbed with a stiif brush—but the feel, the smell of damp earth is an essential thing. I don't mind the inconvenience of dirt.

As I tug up a strand of ground ivy, a toad hops onto my lap. Befuddled, he blinks bead-eyes, presses flat against my thighs. If I were a witch, I'd dress this most beloved of familiars in a velvet suit trimmed with ribbons and bells. I'd sing while he danced and never think of slicing off a toe for a Weird Sister's brew. Perhaps, I'd collect a few droplets of toad spittle to concoct my invisibility ointment—but I am no witch.

I gently clasp *Bufo americanus*, stroke his cranial crests with a forefinger. These bony ridges *do* look like horns. I can understand why my foremothers thought toads in league with the devil. I don't touch the swollen lumps behind his eyes. Filled with toxic secretions, the paratoid glands are rumoured to cause warts—but warts originate with viruses, not amphibians. I continue to stroke his bumpy head. If he is an elderly toad, this fellow carries a jewel in his skull that's an antidote to poisins. Should I hold a toadstone before his smiling face, he'd leap upon its gray surface, try to possess its magic.

Fay-colored, I believe this thick skinned creature a luck-bringer. Legend holds he could be a dwarf spending daylight hours in toad-shape, or a benevolent dead man visiting his old abode. He might be an enchanted prince shape-changed into a toad rather than his watery cousin. Perhaps he's fallen from the lips of a foul tempered stepsister who insulted a fairy. I think him no dwarf, wraith, or prince, but a charming weather prognosticator.

Kill a toad and it will rain, the old saw goes. There is no need for toadicide. Able to hear distant thunder long before my human ears can detect the rumblings, I just need to witness him making his way to safety to know of a storm approaching.

He watches me as I study him. I've heard his mating calls outside my bedroom window these past few nights. His dark throat expands, contracts, expands as distinct toadsongs fill the star-lit garden. In the haze of the waning moon, I've felt a kinship with his soft-bellied eroticism, his warm June fertility.

I place the toad back in the underbrush beside a rhododendron's trunk. He gazes at me from beneath half-closed eyelids. I glance at the sterling toad-ring circling my third finger. Temporary replacement until my engagement ring is repaired, it slips round and round, clicking against my wedding band. I pick up a smooth clear pebble from in front of his green-brown toes, slip it into my pocket.

Toadstone, moonstone, or a bit of quartz—it matters not. I will slide this gift underneath my pillow and tonight as his sensual singing lures a female to the sweet woodruff, I will press aginst my husband. Warm and close in the muggy dark, man and woman will celebrate our place in the universe, our beginnings in the primordial swamp.

§ § §

Vonnie Winslow Crist *of Jarrettsville, Maryland is an artist, poet and writer. Her poems, stories and illustrations have graced numerous regional and national magazins with several stories receiving awards. She has authored two books: ESSENTIAL FABLES (Lite Circle Books, 1996) and Leprechaun Cake & Other Tales—A Vegetarian Story-Cookbook for Children (The Vegetarian Resource Group, 1996). Call 410-557-0177 for information on either book. She is currently one of the Literary Arts Advisors on the Maryland Arts Council and a participant in the Poets-In-The School program.*

Rules

by

Donya Currie

I'm leaving room for you here in my living room—you can bring in a coffee table if you want, and there's space for your coat in the front closet. Put your boots on the floor next to the umbrellas.

You can have one of the bedroom closets and two refrigerator shelves. The top right dresser drawer is for your socks and underwear. T-shirts go in the bottom drawer next to mine.

I cook on Mondays and Wednesdays and you cook on Tuesdays and Thursdays and we eat out Fridays. Weekends we'll leave open. Pasta reheats well.

You clean the bathroom and I take out the garbage. I do the dishes and you vacuum. Change the answering machine to give both our names. You can put a joke on there, too, but don't make it too long because people get impatient and might not want to leave a message.

Keep your cat away from my fish tank, at least the top. She might be able to pry open the cover if she tries hard enough.

Shave often so you don't scratch my face when we kiss but don't leave whiskers in the sink, and keep the toilet lid closed. That's an Ann Landers solution to the seat up-seat down dilemma. The last one to bed has to check the front door lock and turn off the lights. Dont forget the small one over the stove. No Metallica after 10 p.m. because Mr. Hansen downstairs will call the landlord. Keep the bills in a stack by the phone.

Whoever drinks the last beer has to buy more, at least a six-pack, and Bud Light is not a substitute for Foster's. Squeeze the toothpaste tube from the bottom and flatten as you go up. Always say, "I love you" before you go out because it could be the last time we see each other. Wipe your feet.

When your mother comes to visit, she sleeps in our bed, I sleep in the guest room bed and you sleep on the couch. That way you will be the one caught in the groggy, unarmed state of half-awake when she creeps past the living room into the kitchen to make coffee and then makes so much noise looking for a spoon you have to get up and answer her questions about why were not married. *Yet.* We take her to the church across the street Sunday morning even though we hardly ever go there. The minister is so friendly he'll act like were regulars. Your mother loves the choir for the way they sing "How Great Thou Art."

Empty the dishwasher when you notice its full of clean dishes. Look at the magnet on the outside to check. "Clean" means its time to empty, obviously. Mop the kitchen every other week. Don't leave half-filled glasses on the table. Always use a coaster.

You never say, "You look fat," and I never say, "You drink too much." Think it all you want, but never say it. Never show it on your face, either. When we dance together late at night for no reason, turning the living room into a ballroom, you can pick the music. If you let me decide, I will choose Van Morrison, the entire "Moondance" album. Hold me extra close during "Into the Mystic."

Sex is out of the question when I have my period. This is only negotiable if you join me in the shower, where you are careful not to bang my head against the tile wall. Passion is great, but I don't want a concussion.

You clean the litter box and I feed the fish. Not too much damage can be done from cleaning the litter box too often, but the fish could die from overfeeding. I learned this early in life, so trust me. My first goldfishs name was Golda.

If you meet someone else, never bring her home, even if I'm away for the weekend. I would be able to smell her on the sheets. But call if you'll be out all night.

I buy bagels every Sunday and you pick up the dry cleaning. Do not lie about where you go after work. Always use condoms and make sure to check the expiration date. Don't love anyone else. You tell me stories about your childhood while I cook, I play guitar for you while you read.

When you move out, leave the toothpaste. You can buy a new tube. Forward your mail and send me sympathy flowers so I can chop off their heads with scissors. My girlfriends will tell me I'm strong and brave. You get on with your life.

Pretend you don't notice the bad job I've done of cutting my own hair when we meet at a mutual friend's party. You can drink as much beer as you want, but I'll drink wine because it has fewer calories. Only white wine. Introduce me to your new girlfriend, but only if she isn't as pretty as me. I won't tell you about my counseling sessions because that is too personal, and I'll have stopped going anyway.

Come to my funeral, but bring daisies, not roses. Men always think women want roses. Daisies are my favorite flower, and roses are pretentious and way too expensive. Stay after all the other mourners leave and put the daisies tenderly on my fresh grave. Softly sing "Into the Mystic." Think of me. Then sing "How Great Thou Art." Call your mother.

§ § §

Donya Currie *works as a computer consultant and freelance writer in Washington, D.C. and recently completed the graduate program in fiction writing at Johns Hopkins University. Her fiction has appeared in Gargoyle and WordWrights. She lives in Alexandria, Virginia with her husband and their daughter.*

ON THE ROAD TO MECCA

By

Rosie Dempsey

As a child I sat on my father's shoulders at the Parthenon because I had lost my shoes and the stones were hot, ate croissants around a pension breakfast table in Paris, rode a sled on slick stones in Madeira, and hardly remembered it all because I was four and half years old. But, I do remember vividly that I almost drowned in the ocean liner pool on the way to live in the Far East. I held tightly to the step railing and floated under the uninterrupted mediterranean sky. There was barely anyone in the pool until a woman lowered herself in and with her bulk bumped my hands off their hold on the tubular railing of the ladder. I distinctly remember sinking to the bottom of the pool and lying there beneath eight feet of water wondering if anyone was going to notice what had happened to me. The next thing I remember is throwing up into a terry cloth jacket strewn across my mother's lap as someone hit my back.

When you are little you think everything that happens to you happens to everybody, that it's supposed to. That's what I thought. I thought I lived an ordinary life, then after awhile, that I was lucky to have adventures. It bred a deep sense of curiosity in me. But, by the time I was nine, I realized that the things that were happening to me didn't happen to everybody, and that maybe these were the things that recognized me as special, for special I wanted to be.

When I was eight and nine years old I lived in Saudi Arabia on the road to Mecca. The buses would breakdown in the front of our house. Men would loiter around the bus outside our compound, their backs against the 12 foot high wall that ringed me in and them out. The yard was dusty atop a hard packed sand, the compound walls were stucco over cinder block. Glass was embedded into the top of the wall in a half-round mound of cement. Shards of clear Coke and green 7-Up bottles were contrasted with colors from odd bottles, including a few shards of royal blue Malox.

Our landlord, Mr. Kandeer lived next door in an adjoining compound. During the two years I lived in Saudi Arabia I played with his two daughters, Mina and Farona, several times a week. I went to their house through a metal gate door in the wall between our compounds which was left unlocked during the day. We would play and watch Mickey Mouse on TV which came on after the Koran in the afternoon. I could hear the prayers from the minaret floating on the 110 degree air several times a day. It was dry heat and bearable as long as you had shoes on.

Sometimes I would go through the metal door, raised up in the wall off the ground, to find the girls and instead find their father, Mr. Kandeer. He would lead me to a cool interior windowless room in his house, where he had a gray metal desk and a tall metal cabinet which he kept locked. Occasionally he would unlock the cabinet doors and give me a writing pad or a candy bar. This excited me because there were no corner stores or shops that I could go to, and other than the occasional visit to the bazaar with my Mother, certainly no place I was allowed to walk to.

When we went to the bazaar, beggars would surround the car, calling for our pity with outstretched hands. Their hands were deeply creased, their clothes dirty and ragged. I wanted to be able to give them something, but my mother would tell me to roll up the window. The bazaar had covered open corridors of shops and vendors hawking their wares. A few times we went to a dressmakers to get handmade matching dresses for me and my two baby sisters. Bolts of cloth lined the bazaar shop wall, floor to ceiling. I would stand on a big wooden counter in a full slip and they'd measure me. I hated the tailor touching me with his thumb hanging off the edge of the measuring tape. As I looked out from my towering viewpoint towards the big front windows, I would see the store clerks from across the shop, their bodies still and arrested in a moment in time as their dark eyes glowed at me. I was embarrassed and saw too that my mother was oblivious to it all.

Mr. Kandeer was not oblivious, he made me feel special. Sometimes he would invite me to stay with him and eat the candy bar he had just given me. In the cool inner room in his house he would sit in the chair and we would talk, facing each other, me sitting on the top of the desk in front of him. Or, he would give me a scrap of paper with his signature on it that I would take to the compound on the other side of his house to where his dress shop was. I would take it to the old turbaned man who sat outside on a chair. Next to him was a big rectangular, red vat on stilts with a bottle opener on the side. Inside the cold water, ice chunks would bump my hand as it went in to pick among the sodas. There was Fanta in grape and orange, 7-Up and Coke. I would roll the tall glass bottle across my head and arms.

I would get this great treat, not a cold soda anywhere that I knew of except at Mr. Kandeer's dress shop, because I would hand the little scrap of paper with Mr. Kandeer's signature on it to the old turbaned man who spoke not a word of English.

Once I wandered into Mr. Kandeer's dress shop, and while looking at the dresses laced with gold, ornate cloth with simple cuts, the store keeper who spoke no more than a few words of English caught me holding a dress in a caress in front of me, as I modeled it facing the dressing booth mirror.

He took the dress from me and hung it up and then he came back to me, pushing me with his gestures into the dressing booth, telling me with his eyes that I was in trouble, as he sandwiched me against the mirror with his body. I could feel a bulge against my chest from his thing between his legs. I squirmed and he backed away as I pushed him, and I ran out of the shop and past the turbaned guard. I never went into the dress shop again, only going to get my Coke on the outside, where I felt safe with my piece of paper with Mr. Kandeer's name on it pressed into my palm.

Maybe I only got the treat if his daughters weren't around. I don't remember. Perhaps I went knowing no one else was there just to see if Mr. Kandeer would offer me a treat, to see his smile shine on me.

One time after I had been there nearly two years, Mr. Kandeer offered to give me a special treat. I went with him, wanting whatever treat he would offer me and delighted in his continued interest in me. We walked to the compound on the other side where his dress shop was. As we walked he told me I was dark enough to be a Saudi girl, which I liked, and that my husband would be a lucky man, which I didn't like. I was confused when we passed the Coke vat which was locked up, and relieved to see that the man who ran the dress shop was not about. He took me up the adobe colored steps that ran along the outside of the building that went to a second floor. They were concrete and tan stucco matching the yard and the walls, in contrast to the endlessly blue sky.

I had never been to the upstairs room and I was surprised to find it completely empty except for a big safe, almost as tall as I was, against the inside wall towards the middle of the long room. I had never seen a real safe before. The pleasantly cool and dusky room enfolded me in my light blue shorts that covered sturdy, straight legs several shades darker than the tan walls, and a t-shirt dusty from playing.

We stood in the room in silence for a moment, Mr. Kandeer leaning against the safe as I stared at it. Then he said, "come over here and sit, on my lap," and he hopped onto the safe and sat cross-legged on top of it, as I had sat many times on the desk before him back at his house.

His face glowed in the dusky light at me from across the room. I knew he shouldn't have been asking me this. "I don't want to, I want to leave."

He pleaded to me "only two minutes, only two minutes."

"I'll scream if you don't let me out right now."

He glanced at the one small high window and I followed his eyes to see that it was closed. He sat there looking at me as I stood ten feet from him staring at the door. I remembered that he had used a key on it when we had entered and then shut the door and put the key in his pocket.

"I'll kill myself if you don't let me out." I hoped to scare him as I thought about how to escape, about how to make him do what I wanted.

"Ha, no, you're a smart girl, you wouldn't do that."

I backed up a few steps to the farthest edge of the room, as if he wouldn't move towards me as long as I kept him in my sites. He was wearing the traditional Saudi silky cotton shirt-dress with slits on the sides and gathered pants, and from the breast pocket he pulled a pack of American cigarettes and began to smoke as though he had all the time in the world. He was even darker than I was and his skin glowed like oil. He uncrossed his legs, and his slippered feet dangled against the front of the safe. He stared back at me.

"Please, only two minutes, only two minutes." I knew I would have to do something since my bluff had failed, and besides how could I get to the window to jump out.

I refused his mantra-like begging "only two minutes, only two minutes," worried about the outcome but also infused with a certain sensuous delight at the affect I seemed to have over him. I knew I had to get out of the room, and I told him "not here, I don't like it here." He agreed to this as if it was a reasonable request and getting off the safe, he opened the door with the key in his pant pocket. I walked out behind him feeling that I had at last gained the upperhand, and as we passed the empty soda vat I darted past him to the outer gate to the street. It opened and I ran along the outside walls of the compounds, to my own entrance on the far side. Almost at my gate, as I turned to see if he had come after me, I fell and scraped my knee badly on the gravelly road. I remembered thinking it was just as well because it would camouflage my upset if I ran into my mother.

No one was about as I made my way to my bedroom on the far side of our house from Mr. Kandeer's. French door windows opened to a balcony that ran around that side of the house. I lay on my bed breathing heavily from running, my heart pounding at the thought of my escape and what had just happened. I called to my brother Michael as he passed my open door and told him conspiratorially what Mr. Kandeer had asked. He sat beside me thinking about it and said, "You better not tell Mom, you'll get into trouble."

"I'm never going to get married," I said and with that Michael left me there, as I looked through the fench doors at the blue squares of sky, and worried about getting in trouble.

Around me lay rolled up carpets in preparation for our unplanned departure from Saudi Arabia. A week later I heard a bomb go off in the distance, and saw the hole in the embassy wall where we usually went to swim in the pool. I had spent the formative years of ages eight and nine on the road that lead to Mecca, and now I was to leave like the pilgrims who passed by in the buses. It was 1967 and the Six Day War was about to start.

We returned to America and I got a new bedroom. I slept on the edge of the world, tethered to my family's house by a one single wall, exposed to the lush backyard, its darkness, its noises. I would steel myself against the strange noises and languish in the ones I knew, like the birds at dusk and dawn, when they could be so loud as to wake me up, and the wind through the jungle of trees that ringed the yard. When I was scared, I'd hold my breath, as I did when we lived in Saudi Arabia. There, my brothers had been home with us for the summers, after being at boarding school most of the year and they would play games on each other and me.

They would build tents over their beds with broom sticks and blankets, build mazes with overturned chairs, made dark with blankets over the top. I would crawl through the maze, and as the youngest it was easier for me to navigate than my bigger brothers.

I always liked the comfort and safety of another body next to mine. My oldest brother Steven says I used to crawl into bed with him sometimes and that I would push so tight to him to fill the crevices between us. We all really only lived together for the first four and a half years of my life and then we lived in different countries. Only Michael and we three little girls were with Mom and Dad year round, the rest at boarding schools in different countries.

On these summer visits my brothers would come in when I was going to sleep, quietly crack open the door, crawl along the floor, and pop up next to my bed with a surprise yell. I'd come to screaming and bawling and my brothers would be laughing. And of course, I'd stop making a fuss immediately, mad to have been tricked, wanting to make out I hadn't been surprised at all.

So later back in America when my cousin Terry, Aunt Mable's second oldest son, surprised me by coming into my room at night, I thought it was the same thing, a game I should try and win at, something else I was supposed to follow along with, or figure out if I was the smart girl I liked to think I was.

Terry and my Aunt Mable had come back with us after we had visited them in Long Branch the summer I was eleven. Aunt Mable went home after a week and Terry was to stay out the month. He wasn't loud and boisterous like most of the family. He mostly hung out with my older brothers, but one time I got to go with them when they went downtown to tour the FBI.

The boys all slept in the attic and there was no bathroom up there, so Terry must have come down to use the bathroom and come through my sisters open door, their room led to mine. I woke up with him standing over me. I didn't recognize him at first but he said "sh" with his finger to his mouth and I knew it was him. He sat on the edge of the bed, and I asked what was wrong, he said he couldn't sleep, it was very late at night.

As he sat on my bed, without saying anything, he lifted my cotton gown and I could feel the late summer breeze coming through the windows as it pushed into and fluttered the fabric of my nightgown. I could not see his body or his hands, my gown obscured most of him from view, as its length was spread high and wide. And I thought about how much this felt like going to the dressmaker's shop at the bazaar, knowing that eyes were intently upon me.

And then as if the measurements were taken, down my gown came. He smiled at me and held my hand promising that when I came up to his parent's house the next summer he would take me to the boardwalk at night to play the arcades, as long as I didn't tell anyone he came to visit me. We were to be special friends and I liked this. I did think it was odd, but I didn't care because I had always wanted to go to the arcade at night.

I wondered if he was lonely like me. I thought I could help him by being friends and understanding his need for company. I was eleven, he was sixteen. I had been to his parents house just twice, but he always showed an interest in me and had even taken me to see a baseball game at night.

I lay in bed listening to the night sounds alive with awakeness and felt as though a glow must be coming off me like a shining ray from heaven. Is this how Jesus felt to be chosen? Yes, there would be a place for me now, I knew it. The world would make room, extra air would be added, now that he had made a secret with me, not anyone else, special things would come to me.

I told my best friend Suzi the next day after church. We decided he was weird, but okay. This thing would be mine alone away from the parents and their power over me. Besides, how could I ever tell my mother that her favorite sister's, favorite son was bothering me in the night?

My plump softness gave me a femaleness of flesh and I couldn't wait to be older like my brothers and sisters. And yet, I did not understand this lifting of the nightgown, other than his curiosity. He did come to me one more time. But this time when he lifted my night gown, he touched the brown nipples on my chest. I didn't even wear a bra yet, but I was very conscious that some girls my age did. I bet none of them had someone touch their nipples. He reminded me he'd take me to the arcade, and not to tell anyone, and that more exciting things would happen to me as I got older, and I found that a dizzying prospect. As he left, his hands brushed me and I got goosebumps. Behind him the dark windows framed his reddish-blond hair and his smiling face.

As he tiptoed away, my door squeaked and then I heard the attic door close. I lay on my bed against the radiator, the big book shelves set onto it. My terrarium with my miniature frog that I found in the woods, sat on the bottom shelf. And then my door squeaked open and my cat, Gregora, walked in as my heart raced not knowing who would be behind him, knowing I could be in trouble for what had just happened, that somehow it could all be my fault. But Gregora jumped on my bed, not followed by anyone, he settled in on my pillow as I reached my arm up to pet him to sleep.

This time I didn't tell my best friend Suzi because I knew he wasn't suppose to touch me, but there didn't seem to be any harm.

When I went to sleep each night before he left our house I would listen very carefully to hear if the attic door would open so he couldn't surprise me. I intended to be awake if he came into my room again. I didn't like being caught unawares.

The year was 1969, society was transforming and Vietnam was happening. I was eleven years old and experiencing my own sexual revolution.

§ § §

Rosie Dempsey *of Washington, D.C. is a publicist in the health field, and a writer of fiction and non-fiction. Her essays and short stories have been published in The Washington Post. and The Cleveland Plain Dealer. She was a 1998 finalist in both the Larry Neal Writers' Award and in the New Letters Literary Awards. She is currently at work on a novel.*

SPARROWS IN RAIN

by

Barbara Westwood Diehl

They all call me Mommy, except Jerome. He calls me Miss. Jerome is a neighbor kid, almost a son to me. He lives in the little brown house with broken steps on Lemmon Street. His yard touches mine through the wire fence.

Jerome was at my house yesterday with some younger brothers and a sister. The little ones said, "I'm hungry, Mommy," so I gave them applesauce, cheese, and graham crackers. They sat on my back steps to eat, balancing plastic bowls and paper plates on their laps. Jerome watched them as they settled down, then sat down on the bottom step, slouched, banging his bony knees together.

"Have you had lunch?" I asked him.

"I had noodles last night."

"Did you eat some cereal this morning?"

"No, I didn't have no lunch."

"Cereal is breakfast, Jerome. Breakfast is what you eat in the morning. Lunch is middle of the day. Dinner is what you eat at night."

I always feel like I'm doing the ABCs or times tables with Jerome. All right, Miss, he says. But I don't think I'm getting through.

"Are you hungry?"

He shrugged his knobby shoulders, and I went ahead and gave him lunch. Plus sugar wafers because I wanted to see him eat them.

After he ate the applesauce, cheese, and graham crackers, he bit into a sugar wafer. It looked papery and dry on his lips.

"Well, do you like it?" I leaned forward with the open package, ready to pull out more wafers if he liked them.

"Is this lunch?"

"This, I suppose, is a dessert." I crumpled the cellophane closed and got up to put the wafers away in my cookie tin. "I thought you'd like them. They were supposed to be a treat."

"All right, I'll have some of them cookies." And he let me give him some. Then his little brothers and sister climbed the steps crying, "Can I have cookies, Mommy? Can I have cookies too?" I filled their hands.

Jerome ate a couple of sugar wafers for me and said, "They're all right, Miss." But they made him look ridiculous when he tried to smile for me. I gave him two glasses of milk to wash them down.

I told him, "You're all right, Jerome," and let him go.

The children stepped carefully around my flower beds and climbed over the fence into the yard of clothesline and broken toys. The wire fence sags from the weight of children full of applesauce and sugar wafers. It sags first toward Shari's house, then toward mine.

Tomorrow, on the way to Cascade Lake, Jerome and I will stop at Snyder's Produce and peel back the husks and silk of Silver Queen corn. We will hoist honeydew melons, too, guessing how green and sweet inside. The fruit and vegetable stand on the way to the lake will be sturdy and made of weathered wood, bright with salvia and sunflowers. The peaches will be soft and ripe, the tomatoes firm and red. This is what I want, for us.

A farmer's wife will hand us paper bags. Maybe she will be a little fat and wear an apron. I think she should have an accent, maybe German. She should smell like hay. Because I will buy Jerome a loaf of raisin bread with thick white icing on the top, he will smile for me. I'd like to see his eyes light up.

I should get some rest before our trip, but I can't. One of my three tall windows is open to let the paint smell out, so I can hear the gunfire and radios. A helicopter drones over the roof. It sweeps close enough to rattle the window, loud, louder, rumbling louder, until I think there must be armed men on my fire escape. Then it goes away, the roar muffling down to a hum, and I think it must be way to the west. A knife fight, maybe, or kids bailing out of a stolen car. Then no, here comes the engine buzzing the roof again, and my heart pounds. Search beams sweep the sky and my bedroom walls.

Then bottles hit the sidewalk and rain glass into the street. I worry about my car, and hope the patch of impatiens I planted around the tree out front will be all right.

I worry about Jerome, back there on Lemmon Street, but I think that somehow he will be all right. In the morning, his mother, Shari, will awaken groggily on the sofa bed and find her crying baby in the stroller in the kitchen. She will lean over the sink, all her scrawny weight on her elbows, and wait for the water to get warm so that she can mix it with a scoop of formula and prop the bottle with blankets. Then there will be quiet for a while. Upstairs, Jerome will wake up on a bumpy mattress and rise from a warm tangle of younger brothers and sisters. I can see him waking up very slowly, eyes opening under heavy lids and lashes, his skull propped on a skinny neck. Like his mattress, Jerome is bumpy and torn, all knobs and joints, scraped up and scabby. I can see how he works, what makes him tick, like a clear glass clock.

Lemmon Street is my alley. That's where I put out trash in metal cans and pull up weeds from the cracks in the concrete. Looking down from my kitchen window, the houses on Lemmon are boxes drawn with a fat wobbly pencil, empty squares for windows, a rectangle for the door, crayon-colored over the lines, unfinished, as if a child had drawn them.

Cars don't go by much. Sometimes a boyfriend of Shari's drives by in a beat-up Lincoln. He can pound his fist on her door without getting out of the car. You can hear him, bam, bam, through the walls and over yards of clotheslines and broken toys up to the big houses on Lombard Street where the renovators live. Where I live. After a long-minute of him pounding, bam, on that splintered door, Shari will drape herself out the second floor window, digging her elbows into the sill, and say, "huh" or "what" at him. He comes and he goes, like the boyfriends before him, like the children riding rusty tricycles through pint bottles and concrete weeds on Lemmon Street.

In the morning, I can look out my second story window, high above Lemmon, and see Jerome. There is no screen in any of the three windows on the back of their house, and Jerome, and sometimes a younger brother or sister, will lean far out and wave to me. My heart beats like crazy when he does this. I grimace and wave back, screaming, "Don't lean out too far. You'l fall."

Shari is never there when they totter on the window ledge, when they walk through broken glass in bare feet, when helicopters graze the rooftops in search of armed men and the children stare gape-mouthed from the steps at the search beams. Like a sparrow in its nest, Jerome searches the sky wide eyed. His shirt flutters over his ribs.

I have this notion I can make him all right, put meat on his bones, make him be what a kid ought to be. I have this picture in my head of how a kid is supposed to be.

Later yesterday afternoon, I saw Jerome on Carey Street. The temperature yesterday climbed over a hundred, so someone opened a fire hydrant and water gushed into the street. Children tumbled from their hot little Lemmon Street houses and ran to the cold water, screaming, screeching at the cold, pummeled by the spray. They danced, scarecrows in the rain, clothes sodden on their bones.

Soon the fire department man would come with his big wrench, and the water would drain away. Every last drop would steam away. So they splashed and kicked and screamed and let themselves be soaked and pummeled by the river because it felt so good and the fire department man would come soon and wrench it off.

Jerome hung back. A few feet from him stood Shari, smoking, her baby riding on her hip. The little ones who call me Mommy stamped in the fire hydrant river, but Jerome just stood there, watching.

"Get in," Shari said.

But Jerome didn't.

"Go on now," she said again, poking her cigarette toward the street. "Get in there before it's turned off."

But again he wouldn't. He shoved his hands into his pockets. I couldn't catch what Shari said next. The words blended into the screams of the children and the pounding of water on the street. She flicked her cigarette away and yanked him by his upper arm into the tide, then stood there firm in the current with her baby on her hip. Jerome tried to turn back, but she shoved him and he lost his footing.

"Go on and get wet." Shari stood firm and the water parted for her legs. Jerome flopped around, no foothold, no handhold, but Shari just shifted the baby on her hip and waded away. At last he got to his hands and knees, and then to his feet and staggered up. He pulled himself after Shari, not seeing me. His knees ran red.

When he reached her, she grabbed him by his upper arm and headed toward Lemmon Street. Deafened by the water, the screams, my own numbing shame at not being his foothold, his handhold, I could only walk back to Lombard Street, hot and dry.

I told myself, I will take you to Cascade Lake, Jerome, where the water is still and cool like an open hand.

It is time to go and I bang on Jerome's Lemmon Street door, bam, bam—but nothing. No Shari. No baby crying. I bang harder, wait a little bit, then bang again, harder. After long minutes, Jerome hangs out the upstairs window with his "huh" face. I remind him. "Today we go to Cascade Lake."

"Oh." He pauses. "Yeah." Another minute and he comes out the front door fresh from bed. His eyes are heavy with sleep and his hair is uncombed. He has nothing but the rumpled clothes on his back.

"Do you have a towel, Jerome?"

He looks at me like I'm some hovering helicopter flicking search beams at him.

"Do you have a towel inside? A bathing suit?"

He blinks. Do I need to explain, like sugar wafers? We need a common language, points of reference. "Never mind, Jerome." I open the car door for him and buckle him in. On the way, we stop at a K-Mart for a towel, bathing suit, sand toys, and goggles.

We stop at Snyder's Produce, as I had planned. I peel back cornsilk, Jerome peels back cornsilk. He rubs the fuzz on peaches, and I do too. The clerk, a sullen high school kid, stares at us. He probably thinks we'll steal stuff.

I bend to Jerome. "It's all right. You can wander around and look." I peel plastic bags off a roll and fill them with peppers and cucumbers.

"What do you want, Jerome?"

He says nothing, but his eyes flicker over melons and leafy greens, and come to rest on flaky pies oozing peach and cherry and fat turnovers with pastry leaves and vines. The raisin bread doesn't matter now. I want to buy him pies. When we leave, we take an enormous apple turnover in a styrofoam box and honey in a big plastic bear.

At Cascade Lake, we eat our lunch on the sand amid children building castles and moats. When we are full and I think it must be time for Jerome to play, he hangs back. This is ridiculous. I bought a towel and suit. I bought sand toys and goggles like the other kids wear.

"Come on, Jerome. I want to see you play in the water." I take a deep breath. We have come so far.

"I don't want to, Miss. Later."

So I wait, making myself be patient.

But this is ridiculous. It feels like a hundred degrees and the sky is blue. There are children building canal worlds and digging holes to China. There is a lake. A wonderful lake that won't drain away and dry up because some man from the fire department comes with a wrench.

"I want you to go get wet right now, Jerome." I have laid out all his new bright things on our towel. A beautiful bucket painted red, white, and blue. A shiny shovel. And he can only squint at me.

"Sunglasses." I snap my fingers and grin. "That's what you need."

But still he only looks at me and doesn't move an inch toward the lake. The grin makes my face hurt, as if he is leaning far, far out that Lemmon Street window and I am waving back and screaming for him not to fall.

This torn and knobby clockwork boy. I do not know what makes him tick. It wasn't supposed to be this way. I had my plans. I had this notion—but maybe that was all it was. Or maybe just a dream I dreamed because I couldn't go to sleep. I want to knock down your door, Jerome, bam, bam, and go inside.

But all he does is look at me.

Furious, no foothold, no handhold for anyone, I unbutton his shirt and it falls off his shoulders.

I try again.

"And this is sand, Jerome. You don't need shoes." I kneel down to untie his laces and they fall apart in my hands. I stand, plant my feet firmly in the sand, and push him toward the water.

"We came all this way, Jerome. Get wet."

The other children stop patting their castles and stare at us. We are all so still. I don't know what to do. Then slowly, for me, like a swimmer poised to swim mournful laps, Jerome goes out into the lake. I sorrow for myself, letting him go. I cringe on the sand at the boy I cannot make into what a boy should be. What I thought a boy should be. Jerome plods on into the lake and I want to reel him back, but I can't. I don't know what a boy should be.

Then Jerome turns back and grins, runs a hand through the water for me, like, see, it's all right, Miss. And then he wades farther out, up to his waist and higher, until all I see is his head against the sky and shoulder blades like fledgling sparrow wings.

§ § §

Barbara Westwood Diehl of Baltimore, Maryland is the editor of The Baltimore Review and President of the Baltimore Writer's Alliance. Her short stories and poems have appeared in *Thema*, *Negative Capability*, *The Crescent Review*, *Midwest Poetry Review*, *Maryland Poetry Review*, *Rosebud*, *and other publications. She received an honorable mention for short story in the ARTSCAPE '96 literary competion.*

IF ONLY

by

Edward Allan Faine

Karen and I remained the best of friends even after I divorced her older sister. She never failed to call or write once a month, and twice visited me in Washington, once during a Vietnam war protest rally, and again for a week of sailing on the Chesapeake Bay. So when I answered the phone, the slight tremor of her voice on the other end alerted me that something was wrong.

"Ned, I'm pregnant!" The line went silent for a split second. "I need an abortion and I don't have the money to pay for it."

I juggled the phone. "Whoa! Back up a minute. Since when?"

"I'm about four months along."

"What about the guy?"

"He's gone. Skipped town."

"My God...just like the movies. Does Edna know?"

"My mother. Are you kidding? I can't tell her or Daddy." Her voice turned nasal, mimicking her mother. "We told you so. We told you not to hang out at those bars on High Street." Then, wistfully, "I'd never hear the end of it."

"Okay, but have you told anybody...your sister maybe?"

"No. I can't trust her. She'd tell Mom. Listen..." She paused for a moment. "I need at least five hundred dollars. I found a woman who works out of a garage on the other side of town, but I couldn't go through with it. She uses this workbench with a light hung over a rafter on a long cord, you know, the kind they use to fix car engines. Ned, I'm scared. I don't know what to do."

"Karen, calm down! It's 1967. Not the Middle Ages. Aren't there safe places to have these things taken care of?"

"Not in Ohio. I've made at least a hundred phone calls. I finally found a doctor in New York, but he's expensive. It'll cost five hundred dollars. Will you lend me the money?"

"Well...of course."

"Thank you," she sighed, "I knew you'd help. I'll pay you back thirty dollars a month. I know it's not much, but it's all I can afford on a secretary's pay."

"Just pay me back when you can, okay?"

"Sure." She exhaled, long and hard, and then continued. "If only I had found somebody to do it earlier, it wouldn't cost so much."

"Are you showing yet?"

"Nobody at work has noticed except my boss. He asked if had put on weight. I told him the dress I had on made me look bigger, but it won't be too much longer before other people start noticing."

"When do you need the money?"

"I'll let you know as soon as I get it all lined up."

One week later Karen called again. I could tell from the sound of her voice that she'd been crying. "Ned, what am I going to do? I couldn't make arrangements with the doctor in New York. Do you think you might be able to find somebody down there?"

"I don't know anything about this stuff. I wouldn't know where to begin."

"Can't you ask somebody you know? You must know someone?"

"I guess I could, but what the hell do I say?"

"Couldn't you say you have a friend in Ohio who needs an abortion right away? It's got to be done in the next month or not at all. I don't want a baby. Not now! I'd never live it down. Everybody would treat me like a tramp." And she began to cry again.

"Listen, Karen, I'll try. But, honest, I don't know anybody who knows about these things."

I was wrong. The next day I had the names and phone numbers of two doctors in New York, one in Washington, and one in Baltimore. Each came recommended by a friend-of-a-friend, that sort of thing. My sources warned that the doctors might use aliases or refuse to discuss anything on the phone. I couldn't even get them to return my calls.

I had all but given up hope when Doctor "Jones" called and agreed to do the abortion. He gave me specific instructions: Bring five hundred dollars in cash and wait for one hour in the lobby of the downtown Baltimore Holiday Inn. At exactly ten a.m. we were to go to room 503, where he would be waiting. He told me to take her straight home after the procedure. He would be injecting a saline solution in the amniotic sac that would induce miscarriage within as little as ten hours.

I called Karen immediately. "Oh, thank you. I knew I could count on you." I heard the relief in her voice. "When can he do it?"

"Next Tuesday. But, I'm a little worried about this injection that's going to cause something to happen in ten hours. It'll take almost ten hours from the time you're injected until you're home—assuming all goes right. I can get you from Baltimore to Washington National airport by one o'clock. The problem is the afternoon flight to Columbus is at five. That means you're home about seven. That's cutting it close."

"Ned, I know what the doctor is going to do. It's the only thing he can do at this stage, and nothing usually happens until after fifteen hours. I'll be safe."

"But he said ten hours. What if there is a delay at the airport? What if something happens on the plane?"

"Nothing will happen. Please, this is my last chance. Can you wire me the money for the ticket? I'll get the plane for Monday night, return Tuesday. Can you pick me up at the airport?"

"Karen, look, why don't you stay over. You can stay at my apartment—"

"Ned! I want to be at home, in my own bed. Don't you understand?"

"I still think it's too risky for you to fly back right after."

"My girlfriend Charlene will help me. Please, just wire me the money."

I hesitated. No way I could convince her to stay in Washington. Karen could be pigheaded at times. She always seemed to have her way with me, just like her older sister.

"Please, Ned. Please," she begged.

Damn, this was the wrong way to do it. Maybe I could put her up at a hotel. Get a nurse, whatever. Damn. She wasn't going to listen to me now. She had her mind made up.

"Well, all right. I'll wire you the money for the ticket, no problem, but I can't let you fly back by yourself. Anything could happen. I'll fly home with you, and then fly back to Washington. You make sure your girlfriend will be at the airport."

"She will, don't worry."

The trip to Baltimore went without a hitch. We waited in the Holiday Inn lobby for an hour and then went to room 503 at ten. I knocked. No one answered. The door to 504 behind us swung open. Doctor Jones, a pasty-faced man, greeted us and then asked me to come back for Karen at eleven o'clock. For the next hour, I paced the streets of downtown Baltimore; the air so hot and heavy I could hardly think, and that suited me fine. When I returned, the doctor had left and Karen was anxious to leave. Within two hours we were in the Washington airport lounge waiting for our five o'clock flight. Karen fidgeted in her seat with a faraway look in her eyes. With four hours to kill I made small talk to keep her mind off things. I asked about her job, happenings in Columbus, vacation plans and, without thinking, asked, "Would you have thought five months ago you'd be sitting in an airport lounge with me munching salty peanuts and waiting for a plane back to Columbus?"

"No," she replied. "Who would have thought...he really wasn't my type, you know. Ordinarily, I wouldn't have given him the time of day, but Jimmy and I had broken up two weeks earlier, and I was feeling down. I wasn't thinking right. We drank too many whiskey sours at that stinking bar, and then I forgot to use my diaphragm. So..." Her voice trailed off. "Here I am in this damn airport lounge."

"You're going to be all right, Karen." I stopped her remorse. "Someday you'll meet a nice guy and everything will be okay."

"Yeah, right."

We boarded the plane a half hour late and strapped ourselves in our seats. The captain announced another delay due to mechanical trouble. I tried to hide my panic. It had been over seven hours since Jones had given Karen the injection. I remembered his admonition that she could miscarry in ten hours. Beads of sweat formed on my neck and forehead. Damn it, I knew we were cutting it too close. I leaned over to tell Karen, but I changed my mind. I wanted the journey to be over.

After an excruciating two-hour delay, we lifted-off and I settled back into my seat for the one-hour flight.

About mid-flight, a soft moan snapped me to attention. With her eyes closed, teeth clenched, and her face twisted in anguish, Karen writhed in her seat. Her moans grew louder. Jesus, I thought, this can't be happening. What do I do? I unbuckled my safety belt, climbed over Karen, and waved to the stewardess. She pointed to the illuminated seat-belt sign. I ignored her and hurried back to her station at the rear of the plane. "I've got an emergency! I think Karen's about to miscarry."

"Oh, no! We're running into turbulence and the captain said we may have to divert. There's a big storm crossing Ohio now."

"Yes, but—"

"I'm sorry. How serious is it? Can you tell?"

"No, but I think it's just started."

"Let me talk to her. You've got to sit down."

We went back up the aisle together and found Karen gritting her teeth and grinding her feet into the floor. Only the safety belt kept her from falling into the aisle. The stewardess handed me a blanket and pillow from the overhead compartment. "Put the pillow under her feet and cover her up. Make her as comfortable as possible and I'll be right back. I've got to find out if we have an emergency landing option."

Before she left, she calmed several passengers straining out of their seats to get a better look. The plane entered turbulance and started to dip and swerve. Just great, I thought, what else could go wrong?

The lady across the aisle waved at me and said, "Look, there's blood on her legs." It was dark, the color of chocolate.

I'd never seen anything like it.

The stewardess returned and I quickly asked, "Is there a doctor on board?"

"I've checked the passenger list and it doesn't appear so."

"Can't you just get on the PA and ask?"

"I'll ask discretely. You've got to keep calm. We can't make an emergency landing and we can't land at Columbus either. We're diverting to Cleveland. We'll wait the storm out there."

"Geez. Can we move her to a more comfortable seat, like in first-class."

"No. We're in turbulence. If we were to do anything, we would lay her down in the aisle. But we can't take the chance, we could hurt her more than help her. Stay calm Ned...that's your name, right? Mine's Cindy. Let me check one more time to see if there's a doctor on board."

I was far from calm. Karen's muffled screams alternated with open-mouth gasps for air, her arms tensed and shook as she squirmed uncontrollably in her seat. The stewardess returned and asked the lady across the aisle to take a seat at the rear of the plane. Cindy sat down, her face contorted. She chewed her lower lip. She reached across, put her hand on Karen, and shot a concerned look at me, whispering, "She's getting worse isn't she?"

"I think she's having trouble breathing," I said softly.

"Yes, I think so," she replied. "With luck, we'll be landing soon. We've contacted the tower in Columbus and they're in contact with Cleveland. There'll be an ambulance to meet us on the tarmac when we touch down. We'll just have to wait it out. I'll get some towels."

Karen slumped in her seat nearly unconscious. Blood continued to flow down her leg. A rank odor worse than the smell of rotted meat emanated from her lap. Fear seized my stomach like a cramp. Karen looked peaceful—too peaceful. I whispered in her ear, "You'll be all right, Karen, just hang in there." Cindy brought several moist towels from her station and we busied ourselves mopping her brow and wiping the blood off her legs.

The turbulance moderated and the plane settled into a gentle forward roll. The co-pilot came back and said, "Don't worry, an ambulance will be on hand as soon as we touch down. The medics know it's a miscarriage and they'll have the right equipment. Is she all right?"

"I don't know. I think she's fainted."

"It won't be long now. We'll be down in less than ten minutes."

The wheels hit the ground and further tensed my taut stomach muscles. I looked at Karen. She was hardly breathing.

The plane stopped. Two white-uniformed medics climbed aboard with a stretcher. In less than five minutes, they moved Karen's limp body to the ambulance. I followed, climbing in the back. We sped off the tarmac, lights flashing, siren wailing. The medics scrambled about with their instruments. Karen was their only focus, their only reality. I watched, helpless, useless, from afar, like an intern on a training mission, hoping she'd come around. I wasn't there but then again I was. I couldn't believe all of this was happening. "Irregular pulse," I heard one say.

"Damn it to hell! Doesn't look like she's breathing much either. Tell Joe to get the lead out and floor this wagon. And tell him to get on the box pronto and have emergency at the door."

Karen looked ghostly. I had seen that pale death look once before in an auto accident. Maybe she'd be all right once they got her to emergency, at least I hoped to Christ she would. The ambulance doors flew open and a hospital crew brushed me aside and rushed her into the hospital. I collapsed into a waiting-room chair, filled out a mindless form and blanked out for what seemed an eternity. Eventually, a lady clad in a white lab coat said, "I'm Mrs. Babcock. This is Doctor Jeffcoat. Come with us, please?"

I followed them to a small room that smelled of Lysol. I sat across from them at a clean, white formica table. Mrs. Babcock spoke first. "I'm sorry, but we were not able to save Karen. Doctor Jeffcoat will explain."

My chest tightened and my breath stuck painfully at the bottom of my throat. I struggled to say, "Save her?" I was fighting for air in this close room. "Whaddya mean save her?", hoping it didn't mean what I though it meant.

"We did our best," Doctor Jeffcoat said. "She lost a lot of blood. It was a miscarriage with complications. Most certainly there was shock. To have something like this happen at twenty thousand feet is quite frightening. Can you give me some details."

"Details? What are you saying?" I paused. "Is...is she..."

Mrs. Babcock placed her hand on my arm. "We're sorry. Karen is gone."

I buried my head in my hands, dug my fingers into my scalp and shook my head. This can't be happening. How could I let it happen? All I wanted to do was help her. Where did I go wrong? The doctor's voice faded in and out of my frantic thoughts. "Was her pregnancy normal? Had she experienced unusual pains, especially in the last several days?"

"It was normal as far as I knew," I said without thinking.

"I'll know more after the Medical Examiner completes his exam. We'll get together then," the doctor said as he left the room.

"Poor Karen. Poor, poor Karen. How will I ever explain this to her mother? To her sister? To anyone? She didn't deserve this. If only that goddamned plane had taken off on time, if only there'd been a doctor on board, if only there'd been no freaking storm we might have made it."

Mrs. Babcock pleaded, "Please don't blame yourself. I'm sure you did all you could."

Her voice sounded distant to my blood-pounded ears, but I heard what she said. No, I didn't do all I could. How could I? Karen was dead.

I slumped forward, arms outstretched, laying the side of my face on the cool, smooth formica table top. It felt strangely comforting. Mrs. Babcock went on in her professional drone, but all I could think of was Karen. "Could you wait here while I—"

"No. I've got to get out of here. I've got to get some air," I said as I quickly brushed by her into the hall and headed toward the red exit sign. She called after me but I didn't stop. Once outside I ran across the hospital grounds in a fine rain and collapsed on a bench between two large pines. Nobody could find me here in the dark night. If only I had thought things through, maybe it wouldn't have ended this way. God knows I wanted to help. I should've insisted she stay in Washington—should've put my foot down, should've stood up to her for once...been more assertive. Next time I'd do things different. Next time! What am I thinking, next time?

I sat erect on the bench in the coal black, misty night and murmured to myself. “If only...I should’ve...Oh, Christ...if only I could roll back time.”

My chest and throat stung from the sudden rush of air as the misty rain mixed with the tears running down my cheeks.

§ § §

Edward Allan Faine of Takoma Park, Maryland has published many stories and articles in a wide variety of magazines. He is the author of the chapter-picture book series for kids 4-8, *LITTLE NED STORIES* (IM Press), available from Amazon.com, Book Clearing House 1-800-431-1579 or 301-587-1202 (Maryland, Virginia or Washington, D.C.) See back page 224 for information on the LITTLE NED STORIES.

IMPULSE CONTROL

by

Sandy Fleming

In Eleventh-grade English Lit, everything is *ironic*. The other day, before Mr. Sturgess came into class, I asked my seatmates if they were ready for their daily recommended allowance of irony. I only got a few scattered chuckles out of that one, and most of them came from the girl behind me—Susan I think her name is. Susan doesn't say much of anything, so I never know if she's laughing with me or at me. She's either a stuck-up, little snot or someone who's incredibly shy, but since she's not afraid to laugh, I'll have to go with "snob" for now.

Anyway, you could say I'm the class clown, because nobody else likes to crack jokes. Amanda Graves, the guidance counselor here at Allison Park High, has had a couple of "friendly chats" with me about "impulse control," or not blurting out the first thing that pops into my mind. Yeah, I guess it's a problem, but I bet if I were a guy, people would laugh more. Boys are supposed to be jokers. If they're loud and obnoxious, that's funny. When I'm loud and obnoxious, I'm just loud and obnoxious.

"You know, Liz, the way you carry on, it's not very *feminine*," Mom tells me. "Boys don't like girls who are loud."

When I remind her that my best friend, my *only* friend at school and probably in all of Pittsburgh is a guy, she raises an eyebrow and says, "Lyle?"

Well, Lyle is my buddy, but he doesn't belong to that category of hormone-crazed adolescent boys that my mother thinks I should be attracting. He's one of these brainy kids who keeps getting pushed ahead several grades at a time. Although he swears to me that he's turning fifteen next month, I'd be willing to bet that he isn't a day over fourteen. I'm not even five-three, and Lyle only comes up to my shoulder. He wears his straight blond hair hanging over his face because he thinks it makes him look older. His voice hasn't even changed yet. But he's a really nice guy and he's pretty mature for his age, whatever that is.

"Lyle, do you think I'm butch?" I ask him while we're eating lunch in the cafeteria. It's the end of sixth period, and the room is practically empty. We are sitting in our usual spot at the round table in the far corner, and sunlight is streaming in through the high windows, beating down on my back and hitting Lyle square in the face, but his hair is in his eyes, so I guess he doesn't care.

He squeezes some ketchup onto his fries. "Butch?"

"Yeah. My mom thinks I don't act feminine."

"I dunno." He shrugs. "I mean, you're not all prissy like some girls, but I wouldn't say you were butch."

I take a bite out of my whole-wheat-pita-and-sprouts sandwich and stare intensely at his fries. "Mom and I were at Macy's last night, and my dress is still there."

The dress in question is lime green with sequins and taffeta and a slit up the side and a super-low-cut V-neck. It's identical to the one Nastida Boom Boom wears in her latest video, where she reaches out of the TV screen and slaps her boyfriend. It's also got a $350 price tag and a "you're-out-of-your-mind-if-you-think-I'm-going-to-buy-you-that-dress" ruling from Mom.

Lyle shakes his head. "I can't believe you're still obsessing on that."

"But it would be THE PERFECT DRESS to wear to the autumn dance," I tell him. "And I bet it would get Greg Daniels' attention."

Lyle wrinkles up his nose at the mention of Greg. He's told me several times what a stuck-up jerk he is, but with looks like Greg's, who cares? I'd at least like the chance to experience his jerkiness first-hand and decide for myself.

"Have you even tried the dress on?" Lyle shoves a tangle of french fries into his mouth. "You'd probably look ridiculous in it. Nastida Boom Boom is ten years older than you and half a foot taller."

"I have one thing to say to you," I tell him, eyeballing the fries.

"Liz, don't!" he pleads, holding up his hand like a crossing guard. "I'm willing to share."

"Castration."

"Oh here, take them." He shoves the fries away. It only works if I remember to wait until he's put the ketchup on them.

"I know how I can make Mom buy me the dress," I tell him. "Remember my cousin Jordan and the baseball cards? How he told my grandparents he was gay so they would buy him a set of baseball cards?"

Lyle brushes his hair out of his eyes. "Aren't your grandparents dead?"

"Yeah," I say popping a french fry into my mouth, "but that doesn't mean it wouldn't work on my mom."

"I don't get the logic of it," Lyle says, shaking his head. "I have a hard enough time with your grandparents buying Jordan baseball cards to keep him from turning gay. But I can't believe your mom would be dumb enough to believe you're gay, and then naive enough to think that buying a dress would cure you. That's almost as stupid as you having the hots for Greg Daniels." He stands up and gathers his books. "I gotta run. I hate sitting in the back and not being able to see."

I'm left alone in the cafeteria to ponder Greg Daniels, the senior. Greg Daniels, who's starred in every play the school has put on in the last three years.

Greg talked to me once. Well, almost. I had just walked headfirst into the ladies room door because I was so busy staring at his butt, and when he looked over to hear what the loud thud was, I said, in my best Pee-Wee Herman voice, "I meant to do that."

He kept walking and turned to his super model girlfriend, Vicki (read, Bitchy) and asked, "Is she spastic or what?"

I shove the last of the french fries into my mouth and swear a solemn oath: I will do whatever it takes to get that dress!

From my modest savings and weekly pittance also known as my allowance, I set my plan into motion. Over the next few weeks, I invest in CD's by k.d. Lang and the Indigo Girls. I start buying "oppressionist literature" by the likes of Adrienne Rich and Rita Mae Brown. I get a life-sized poster of Melissa Etheridge at Planet Music and hang it on the ceiling over my bed. Then one Saturday, I take the bus all the way downtown to the Lingua Lambda Bookstore and buy a T-shirt with a big pink triangle on it and a slogan that reads "Silence = Death." As soon as I get home, I ball it up and stick it in the laundry. If this doesn't tip Mom off, I don't know what will. Just for good measure, I tell Lyle to ask for "Lez" instead of Liz whenever he calls my house.

This Wednesday is the One Day Sale at Macy's, and it just so happens that we need a new iron, and they have one on sale for $19.99. The silverstone is flaking off our old one (with a little help from me and my paper clip), leaving little oblong stains on Dad's shirts.

"Can we see if my dress is on sale?" I ask Mom as soon as we step into the mall. "We're going right past Juniors."

"It would have to be one hell of a sale," Mom says.

Sure enough, the dress is marked down, and there are only a few left in my size. I take one off the rack and hold it against myself.

"Two-hundred-seventy-five instead of three-fifty," Mom muses. "Who would have thought you could get such a bargain on something so hideous?"

Mom's one to talk about taste in clothes. Tonight she's still dressed in the outfit she wore to work: rust-colored polyester high waters and a white rayon blouse with a huge bow on the front of it. You'd think she was a brain-dead secretary instead of a CPA.

"But I would look so *feminine* in this!" I say, fingering one of the sequins along the slit down the bustline. "And lately, I've been so confused about stuff."

Mom tilts her head and narrows her eyes. This is going to be a hard sell.

"For the last few months, I've felt like a boy trapped inside a girl's body," I continue. "All I can think about is girls."

Mom crosses her arms and raises an eyebrow. "Go on," she says.

I take a deep breath. "Mom, I think I'm on the verge of becoming a—"

"Becoming a what?"

"A lesbian."

"Uh, huh. And the only thing that can save you is owning this dress, right?"

I clutch the garment against my washboard-flat chest and try to look Mom square in the eye. I'm dimly aware of a sales clerk looming just a few feet behind us. "Uhm, it's not quite that simple, but..."

"If it's a choice between you becoming a lesbian or wearing that dress, I think I'd rather have a daughter who's gay."

A familiar voice behind me says, "Excuse me, but we're having our Best Dressed Lesbian Sale next week."

I spin around and come face-to-face with Bitchy. Her Macy's tag is about two inches from my nose, and she's wearing a skin-tight sleeveless mock turtleneck with matching black mini-skirt.

"Oh, hi, Vicki. You *work* here?"

Mom puts her hand on my shoulder. "I'll let you two girls chat. Catch up with me in Small Appliances when you're done, Lizzy."

I want to slap the smile right off Mom's face, but not half as much as I want to pummel it off Bitchy's.

"Yeah, I *work* here," Bitchy says. "I'm going to need spending money next year for college. You know I got accepted at Brown."

"Brown? As in Brown University?"

"Don't look so surprised." Bitchy brushes a long ringlet of sparkling blonde hair off her shoulder. "Just because I'm beautiful doesn't mean I'm stupid."

I rock back on my heels. "Well gee, you sure had me fooled."

Bitchy snatches the dress out of my hands and holds it up to the light. "Much as I like to make a high-ticket sale, this dress is all wrong for you."

"And why's that?" I ask, stuffing my hands in my pockets.

"For starters, you're not a 24-year-old five-foot nine-inch rapper." She hangs the dress back in the rack.

"So?"

"Do I have to spell it out for you?" Bitchy flares her nostrils. "A short, pudgy, flat-chested redhead is going to look ridiculous in that dress. You're not going to attract *anything* wearing that, *male or female*." She points a long red fingernail toward a wall full of video screens. "You want to feel more feminine, try some of the floral prints on that rack."

"Well thanks a lot," I say, turning to leave. "You've been *so* helpful. And by the way, I'm a strawberry blonde."

"Oh, before you go, Blondie," she says, tapping me on the shoulder, "I just wanted to let you know that I might not be able to keep the little heart-to-heart you had with your mom to myself."

I shrug nonchalantly, but I'm shocked that she believed what I said to my mother, even though it was obvious that my mom saw right through it.

"But you know, Elizabeth, I'm not half the bitch you think I am."

"Really?" My mind is already racing ahead to when she tells the whole school I'm a lesbian.

"No, I'm a double bitch. Do you remember Kimberly on *Melrose Place*? I modeled myself after her."

"Look, nobody's going to believe what you say anyway." I spin around on my heel to make my grand exit. "Now if you'll excuse me, I have to go to Small Appliances."

"I'll bet you do," Bitchy says with a smirk.

The next few days at school are like something out of the *Twilight Zone*. Classmates who never acknowledged my existence are saying "hi" in the hallways. Everybody's laughing at my jokes. People are even sitting next to me in homeroom.

At lunch on Friday, Susan, that snobby girl from English class, almost sits with me and Lyle. She heads straight for us, tray in hand, when she suddenly veers off and sits by herself at another table.

"What's with her?" I ask Lyle. "Is she stuck up, or what?"

Lyle shakes his head. "Not at all. She's really shy. Can't you tell? They have her picture beside the word 'mousy' in the dictionary. She probably wanted to sit with us but lost her nerve at the last minute."

"So why don't you go over there and ask her to join us?" I say, unwrapping my carrot and celery sticks.

"Nah. She might think I'm hitting on her. And there's no way I'm going to leave you alone with my fries."

"So what do you think is going on with everyone else?" I ask him. "Why are people being so nice to me all of a sudden? If they actually believe I'm a lesbian, why hasn't anyone spray painted 'RUGMUNCHER' on my locker yet?"

"I dunno. Maybe it's cool to be gay. Isn't this The Year of the Lesbian or something?"

"I just don't understand it," I say. "One minute, I'm a geek and a freak, and the next minute, people think I'm cool because I'm gay? It just doesn't make any sense. I know Bitchy must be hating life right about now!"

"Maybe this is your fifteen minutes in the spotlight." Lyle tears open a packet of salt. "So when are you going to set them straight, no pun intended?"

"I hope the whole thing blows over...and pretty quick, too." I reach over and snatch a french fry. "Aren't you going to put ketchup on them?"

"Nope," Lyle says. "I'm onto your french fry scam, and when people get hip to this other scam, I'd hate to see what's going to get scrawled on your locker."

"I'm not scamming anyone," I tell him. "I can't control what they say about me. I can't even control what I say about myself."

"But, this whole thing is a lie."

I lean in toward the table. "Keep your voice down."

Lyle gathers his books. "The longer you wait to clear things up, the worse it's going to be," he says, getting up to leave. "And next time, buy your own damn fries!"

"That's no fun." I twirl the empty french fry container on the table.

The next period is English. I'm thinking about what Lyle said when my reverie is suddenly interrupted by Mr. Sturgess.

"I'll give you the benefit of the doubt and repeat myself in case you didn't hear me the first time. Your thesis statement for your personal essay about *The Scarlet Letter*? Sometime today, Liz?"

I look down at my notebook, which is blank. To buy myself some time, I stand up and stare straight ahead at the blackboard, noticing for the first time that it's actually a dark olive green. It has some half-erased notes from the last period, squiggles, slashes, dots…a triangle…

The words fly out of my mouth before I can edit them. "My personal essay about *The Scarlet Letter* directly relates to my personal experience, because, you see, while her scarlet letter was 'A' for 'Adultery,' my scarlet letter is actually pink, and it's a Lambda, and it stands for 'lesbian.'"

There is dead silence. From clear across the room, I hear the ticking of the quartz clock that hangs over the olive blackboard. A pencil drops. Chairs squeak. I have crossed over the line. I am a thoroughly despicable person who will burn in hell for eternity. Thank God Lyle isn't in this class. My fifteen minutes of fame have just run out.

Then it starts, timidly, from the very back of the room and builds like a wave as it washes over me. I drop into my seat like an overstuffed knapsack as everyone else stands and applauds. Students in the hall peer through the doorway to see what's going on.

When the cheering finally dies down, Mr. Sturgess clears his throat and fingers a small piece of chalk. "We all look forward to hearing your essay next week, Liz."

"Your speech was awesome!"

Snobby (or is it mousy?) Susan has cornered me in the hallway after class.

"Uh, thanks," I say, still in shock from the whole ordeal.

She slowly extends her hand, which is limp and clammy. "I just wanted to shake your hand. You're so brave to come out like that in front of everyone."

"Uh-huh." I shift from one foot to the other and get a good look at her for the first time. Long brown hair parted in the middle and thick, round glasses. Lyle was right. How could I have mistaken this girl for a snob?

"I mean," she stammers, "I can barely get up the nerve to say 'hi' to anyone, so I really admire what you just did. Not that I wasn't impressed with you before. I've always thought you were hilarious."

I raise my eyebrows.

"I meant that in a good way," she says. "Uhm, look, I don't want to make you late for class or say anything stupid, so I'll let you go."

"You're worried about saying something stupid to *me*?" I ask. "I always say stupid things. I wouldn't mind somebody else doing it now and then."

"What you said today in class wasn't stupid," she tells me before she walks away. "It was pretty heroic."

It's Monday morning, and the only clean top I have is the pink-triangle "Silence = Death" t-shirt.

"You're sixteen," Mom says to me over her steaming cup of coffee. "You know the rules. If you don't help with the family's wash, you are responsible for your own. If I remember correctly, you haven't gone anywhere near the laundry room in about two weeks."

I hold out the t-shirt. "So how did this get washed when nothing else of mine did?"

Mom peers up at me from over her glasses. "I must have mistaken it for one of your father's undershirts." She takes a sip of coffee and smiles. "Lucky for you that you've got a clean shirt to wear."

I sigh and roll my eyes.

"Smile, it's the Year of the Lesbian." She toasts me with her coffee cup.

"Guess that makes me one lucky dike," I mutter as I leave the kitchen.

At school, everyone is waving to me, calling my name, complimenting me on my shirt. In homeroom, Lyle takes one look at me and whispers, "I thought you were going to lay low on this until it all blew over."

"That was the plan," I say, tugging on the bottom of the shirt, "but it was the only clean thing I had to wear, thanks to Mom. She thinks this whole thing is a riot. And I didn't even tell her about *The Scarlet Letter* thing on Friday—"

Just then, the P.A. system crackles to life with the morning announcements and Bitchy's perky voice resonates through the school. "Who decided to let Bitchy do the announcements anyway?" My voice is loud and angry. "Who crowned her Queen Shit of Turd Island? Just because she got accepted at Brown University—"

Lyle shushes me and points to the speaker.

"I know this isn't standard procedure," Bitchy enthuses, "but I have some classmates here who have something *very* important to say to the entire school."

After a moment or two of fumbling microphone clicks and flutters, a shaky male voice announces, "My name is Josh Reed, and I'm gay."

Homeroom erupts into cheers. The next speaker is a girl.

"I'm Kathy DeLuca, and I'm a lesbian."

More clapping and cheers. Lyle and I look at each other, dumbfounded.

"I just wanted to say that I would not have had the strength to come out if it wasn't for tenth-grader Liz Hawkins," Kathy continues. "Her courageous announcement in English Lit on Friday inspired me to take a hard look at myself and at the lie I was living."

Everyone in homeroom is applauding; some are yelling, "Way to go, Liz!"

Lyle pats me on the back and I bury my face in my hands.

Kathy finishes her speech with "Today, I am proud to say that I am gay, and gay is okay!"

My entire homeroom begins chanting and pounding on the tables, "Gay okay! Gay okay! Gay okay!"

"Did you want to talk to Liz?" Lyle asks.

It's the end of sixth period, and Greg Daniels is hovering just a few feet away from our lunch table.

"Yeah," Greg says, "but I kind of wanted to talk to her alone, if that's all right with you."

"Sure." Lyle says, backing away from the table. "I was just leaving."

Greg pulls a chair up next to me and I just sit there, stunned. First, because he's come to talk to me. Then, because he's not as handsome up close. His nose is larger than I thought, and his eyes are kind of small and far apart.

"Mind if I ask you a personal question?" he asks, moving his chair even closer. Our knees are touching.

"A personal question?" I feel like my face is just a few inches away from a blast furnace, but I rest my chin in my hands to look casual. I'm not sure I like him sitting so close.

"Uhm, are you a virgin?" His breath smells like fish sticks, and there's a whitehead on his chin that looks like it's about to explode. I move my leg away from his.

"What ever happened to introductions?" I ask. "Like, 'Hi, I'm Greg Daniels. You must be Liz Hawkins. How do you like school?'"

He puts his face closer to mine. "Like, have you ever been with a guy?" I lean back in my chair. "I'm only sixteen. And yes, I'm a virgin, not that it's any of your business." So Lyle was right about this guy.

He leans toward me and squeezes my shoulder. "Then how can you know you don't like guys if you've never tried one?"

I pull my arm away, and he drops his hands to his lap. "I want to show you something," he tells me, shifting sideways in his chair and looking around the room. "Ever seen one of these?"

I glance down just as he's pulling himself out of his jeans. There isn't much there, except for something on it that looks like a big wart.

"You creep! I don't want to see it," I say, scraping my chair backwards. "What about your girlfriend, Vicki?"

His eyes glaze over and then narrow into slits. "Sure, I could probably set up a threesome. I'd love to see you two go at it." He grins and zips up his pants.

I stand up to leave. "I think I'll pass."

Greg gets up and blocks my way. He's a good six inches taller than I am. "Give me a chance, Liz. I'll convert you."

"Thanks, but no thanks," I tell him.

I push past him and rush out of the cafeteria, wondering how I could have ever liked Greg Daniels, or the stupid lime green dress, for that matter.

"I never thought I'd say this in a million years, but I don't like being popular," I tell Lyle over the phone Wednesday night. "In fact, I hate it. I feel like I'm in a glass bubble. Everybody looking at me. Talking to me."

"Not everybody," Lyle says. "There are a bunch of kids in my AP classes who could care less. Not that they're anti-gay or anything. They just don't understand what all the fuss is about."

"Well good," I tell him. "Maybe this will all die down soon."

"Don't be so sure," Lyle says. "Did you know that nine more seniors, four juniors, and a couple of sophomores and freshman came out today—both guys and girls? I can't believe they're all gay."

"I'll bet they're not," I say, twirling the phone cord around my fingers. "Gay must be the flavor of the day."

Lyle says. "Oh, to bask in blessed anonymity!"

"Anything would be better than this," I lie down on my bed and stare up at Melissa Etheridge. "Guys are looking at me like The Final Frontier, and Kathy DeLuca keeps inviting me over her house for slumber parties, except I'm pretty sure I'm the only one on the guest list. And I don't know about that Susan girl."

"Susan's cool," Lyle says. "She told me the reason she never sat with us at lunch before was because she thought we were an item. Can you imagine that?"

I chuckle.

"But there's something else I should probably tell you. Now don't get pissed off," Lyle says.

I sit up. "What?"

"I kind of told Susan the truth, and she wasn't too happy."

"Oh, that's terrific, Lyle. Thanks a lot. What did she say?"

"Just that it was tacky for you to lie about something so personal, and she thinks you must be some kind of gay-basher if you let people look up to you when you're not really gay."

"I hope you at least defended me."

"Of course I did," Lyle says. "I explained to her that your mouth runs at double the speed of your brain, and that you are planning to put an end to this charade and tell everyone the truth."

I flop back down on the pillow and stare up at Melissa again. "Oh, great. And how am I supposed to do that?"

Lyle is quiet for a moment. "Maybe you should have another one of those friendly chats with Amanda Graves," he suggests. "She might have some insight. She's used to dealing with screwed up adolescents—it's her job, after all."

I prop myself up on my elbow. Lyle might just have a point.

Amanda Graves' office is all pastels. The walls are pale pink, the oval area rug in the middle of the room has powder blue and white threads running through it, even the overstuffed beanbag chair is a faint lemon yellow. It's supposed to be the perfect, soothing environment for troubled teens, but I am anything but calm.

"I thought they stopped making bean bag chairs in the seventies," I begin. "And didn't they only make them in earth tones?"

"Amanda," as she tells all the students to call her, is wearing her long dark hair in a French braid. She smiles and gestures for me to sit down. I lower myself into the beanbag chair, my usual seat for our "informal chats."

"I had it re-covered." she says, pulling my file out of her cabinet and seating herself directly across from me on a pink cushion on the floor. She crosses her legs Indian style. The file looks thicker than I remember it from a month ago.

"So the chair is recovered, just like many of your students?" I quip.

"Recovery is a process, not a destination." She smiles and glances into the file on her lap.

"Good thing they make those files expandable, then, right?"

She looks back up, still smiling. "Last time we spoke, we discussed your use of humor to deal with uncomfortable situations, to shield you from potentially painful experiences and feelings."

She must think I made this lesbian stuff up as a joke if she's opening with the humor thing. I nod my head and rub my sweaty palms on my jeans.

"Sounds like you've got the right file," I tell her. It shouldn't be that hard to come clean with her if she already knows. My mind is reeling, thinking where to start.

"I guess you heard about this lesbian business with me," I begin. Already, I'm feeling relieved.

"Yes. You've become quite the item." She folds her hands on her lap and grins. "You're frowning, now. Why is that, Liz? Are you uncomfortable with this role?"

I shift in the beanbag chair. "I'll say. It's like being on display. All of a sudden, people are nice to me and hanging on every word I say, just because they *think* I'm gay—"

Amanda stops me and says, "Don't you see? People appreciate honesty. All they saw before was you hiding behind your jokes. Teens are very perceptive. They know when somebody's covering up. The moment you let down your defenses, open up a little, they accept you for who you are."

I stare down at my lap, the weight of dread burdening my shoulders once again. She hasn't been listening to me. "And what's that?" I ask her.

"Elizabeth Hawkins. An intelligent, funny, caring, honest young person who happens to be gay and isn't afraid of how people are going judge her."

"I was afraid you'd say that," I mumble, staring at the pastel rug. How do I tell her the truth? Where do I start?

"You know, it's perfectly normal to feel this way." She closes my file and gently rests it on the floor beside her. "Many who finally *come out* feel depressed and let down rather than relieved. It takes so much energy to keep up appearances and live the lie, that when the pretense is over, they just don't know what to do with themselves."

"I don't know what to do with myself, that's for sure," I tell her.

"Redirect your energy into positive channels," she says, taking a cleansing breath. "Energize yourself with the goodwill and support of your peers and challenge yourself by taking on a leadership role."

"A leadership role?" I finger the collar of my blouse.

"I know, it's out of your comfort zone, but I think you're up to the challenge. I have something specific I'd like to propose. Now, you don't have to do it just because you think I want you to."

Yeah, right. "Sure. What is it?" I ask, laying my palms open on my lap, trying to look receptive.

"You know about the assembly the school is having for Cultural Diversity Day on Friday?" she begins. I nod.

"In light of everything that's been going on here, I suggested to the Administration that we change it to Cultural and *Lifestyle* Diversity Day, and they were very supportive."

I can tell she's thrilled about it. She usually talks to me in a whispery voice that veterinarians use to soothe frightened pets, but now she's speaking faster and louder and gesturing with her hands.

"Josh Reed and Kathy DeLuca have already offered to say a few words at the assembly, and I think people would love to hear from you." She rubs her hands together. "That is, if you feel up to the challenge."

I look down at my file, thinking that it's going to take up half her office by the time I'm a senior.

"Sure," I answer. "I never met a challenge I didn't like."

It's after 11 P.M. on Thursday night, and Dad has already gone up to bed. Mom and I sit at the dining room table in our flannel gowns and fuzzy slippers. We look like a page out of an L.L. Bean catalog. I've told her all about what's happened, and how the only way I can get out of it is to confess the whole mess to the entire school.

"So what do you think?" I ask my mom as she turns over the last page of my speech. "Will people throw stuff at me?"

"They don't allow food into the auditorium, do they?" she asks, peering up over her reading glasses. "You know this isn't going to be easy, Liz. A lot of kids are going to hate you for what you've done. But I agree, this is probably the only way you're ever going to be able to live with yourself."

I stare at the three double-spaced typed pages. A confession to a heinous crime. The death sentence to my fraudulent popularity.

"It's a very good speech," Mom says. "The people who are your friends will stick by you, and those who don't, probably never really were."

"Yeah, I know." I sigh. "But I just let this whole thing get way out of hand. All because of a stupid dress that I don't even want anymore to wear to a stupid dance that I'm not even going to." I sink down in my chair. "I'll bet cousin Jordan didn't screw things up when he got Grandma and Grandpa to buy him those baseball cards. Why is it that when he told a little fib, he walked away with baseball cards, and the second I start to mess with the truth, my whole world falls apart!"

Mom cocks her head and scratches behind her ear. "It wasn't a fib, Lizzy."

"What?" I sit up in my chair.

"You didn't know your cousin was gay?"

"But he's into baseball and lacrosse..."

"So? That doesn't mean anything. You of all people should know now not to stereotype others." Mom puts her arm around me. "Maybe I've forced you to live too sheltered a life," she tells me. "Maybe I should have started letting you see R-rated movies when you were twelve."

I stare at the table and shake my head. "No, I'd have just gotten myself into worse trouble then."

"It won't be pleasant, Lizzy," she tells me. "and it won't be easy. But in the end, everything will work out."

This is one of those Sensitive Meaningful Mother-Daughter Moments. I belch loudly to break the mood.

The auditorium is packed, and Kathy DeLuca is droning on and on about how she's known as far back as she can remember that she's been gay. I'm sitting in the front row, the sweat from my palms making the paper my speech is typed on translucent. I had volunteered to go last, because I didn't want my bombshell to distract people from the other, legitimate speakers, but now I'm regretting my generosity. I could have been done with it by now.

At last, Kathy finishes, and I shuffle up to the stage and take my place behind the podium.

"Good morning, everyone," I begin. I'm met with loud applause. I hold up my hand to quiet them.

"Please don't clap for me," I tell them. "After you hear what I have to say, I know you're not going to want to applaud."

The auditorium falls silent. I look out into the audience and see Lyle in the fifth row giving me the thumbs up. Susan is sitting next to him, her arms crossed.

"You've all been so nice and supportive these last few weeks that it makes it harder for me to say what I have to tell you." I pour myself a glass of water and take a gulp.

"Many of today's speakers have talked about living a lie. I have been living a lie of another kind, and I owe each and every one of you an explanation, as well as an apology."

I pause to take another sip of water, and people begin to murmur. Do it now, I tell myself. I glance down at my speech, take a deep breath, and gaze out into the audience.

"I'm not gay. It was all a lie," I blurt out.

The audience lets out a collective gasp, and then everyone starts talking to each other at once. I can't hear what they're saying. Nobody looks too friendly.

I wave my hands to get their attention. "Please, let me explain." The auditorium quiets down. "I didn't mean to lie." There are some scattered snorts and chuckles. "It just sort of happened. Somebody misunderstood a conversation I had, and the rumor about me being a lesbian got started. Suddenly, people were acting nice to me. Laughing at my jokes. Saying 'hello'. I mean, this might not sound like much, but I was pretty desperate for attention, so when all this began, I didn't do what I should have done to set everybody straight...no pun intended."

Nobody laughs at the no-pun-intended line. People are shifting in their seats, whispering to one another. I'm losing them.

"The worst part of all this was in English class, when I gave a speech about *The Scarlet Letter*, and how my scarlet letter was lambda. Only, I'm not a lesbian. I'm just a liar."

The whispering in the audience is getting louder, as are the snorts and guffaws. I catch a glimpse of Amanda Graves in the second row, her face an ashen white. By now, I sense that the audience isn't going to pay attention long enough to hear me congratulate them on their tolerance and support of alternative lifestyles.

I continue. "You see, I know this is no excuse, but I kind of have this problem with *impulse control*. Sometimes," I say, stabbing my index finger at my forehead, "I just blurt out whatever comes to mind. There's nothing controlling the flow from my head to my mouth."

The audience groans. People start booing. Somebody throws a crumpled-up piece of notebook paper at me. More follow until I am pelted by a hailstorm of paper balls.

I raise my voice. "I can tell that most of you are really angry, and I can see why. There's no excuse for my behavior. I've let everybody down." I find the last paragraph of my speech and continue from there. "But please don't let my actions take anything away from the very important things that have been happening here. I think it's terrific how accepting everyone has been of their gay classmates. If only society could be more like the students at this school, the world would be a much better place for everyone."

There is scattered applause, but mostly boos and hisses. Lyle and Susan are clapping enthusiastically; Amanda Graves, tentatively; and a good number of students are just sitting there, frowning.

I conclude with, "Stick a fork in my butt, I'm done!"

Nobody laughs at my joke and I scuttle off the stage.

When I walk into the cafeteria sixth period, people in line step back to let me through. I feel like Moses parting the Red Sea. They roll their eyes and turn away. I must be having a bad hygiene day or something.

Lyle is already sitting at our table, as is Susan, who smiles when I pull out my chair.

"I'm surprised you're willing to sit at the leper's table," I tell her. "You know, you're ruining any chance you may ever have of becoming popular in this school." I sit down and begin to unwrap my celery stalks. "Lyle here enjoys being an outcast."

Susan glances at Lyle and says, "Lyle was right about you. He said you wouldn't go on lying, that you would set things right."

Lyle is grinning and nodding.

"And as for forgiving you," Susan continues, "I find it hard to stay angry at someone who's capable of doing something *so* pathetic." Susan puts her hand over her mouth and looks away, trying not to laugh. "I mean, telling your mom if she didn't buy you that dress, you'd turn gay on her." She giggles. "I guess I'll never have to worry about ever saying or doing anything stupid in front of you!"

"Thanks, Lyle. Did you have to tell her everything?"

Lyle shrugs. "I got her to feel sorry enough for you to talk to you. What more do you want?"

Susan folds her hands on the table. "Seriously, Liz, I admire you for getting up on that stage and telling everyone the truth."

"Thanks." I bite into a celery stick. "I suppose this means I managed to make one new friend while pissing off a few hundred others. Now I'll have something good to tell my mom when she asks me what happened at school today."

"So what did Amanda Graves say to you after the assembly?" Lyle asks.

I finish chewing the celery before I answer. "She suggested I volunteer at the Rothman Clinic downtown to help prepare and deliver meals for homebound people suffering with AIDS. You know, to sort of do penance."

"That sounds like a great idea," Susan says.

"Yeah, I'm actually looking forward to doing it," I tell her.

"Oh, I almost forgot." Lyle shoves a basket full of fries in front of me. "I bought these for you. I thought you could use some comfort food today. I hope they haven't gotten too cold."

"Since when have cold fries ever been a problem?" I tell him, stuffing a handful into my mouth. "Thanks."

A balled-up piece of notebook paper hits me on the shoulder and people in the front of the cafeteria start laughing.

Lyle picks it up and throws it at them. "Jerks!" he mutters.

"The kids in this school are so phony," Susan tells me. "At least you know you're full of shit."

"It's one of your endearing qualities," Lyle adds.

"I'll have to remember that for my college interviews."

I look to the front of the cafeteria, where Greg and Bitchy are sitting with a group of seniors. I have two more years here, unless I can talk Mom and Dad into sending me to private school. Of course, I'd probably screw things up there, too.

Greg sees me looking at them and gives me the finger. *Wart Dick!* I think, only I don't say it. Not this time.

§ § §

Sandy Bernstein Fleming *is a graduate of The Johns Hopkins University's Writing Seminars. She was a fiction runner-up in the Artscape '95 Literary Awards Competition, judged by Rita Mae Brown. A later version of that manuscript, Eastern Peaches and Other Stories, was published by Dragonfly Press in December of 1995 and went into a second printing the following month. Another story was published in the Dancing Shadow Review in 1997. Ms. Fleming is a Marketing Manager for the United Communications Group in Rockville, Maryland and lives with her husband Tom and their three cats in Northeast Baltimore.*

The Adjustment

by

John Hayes

The sudden brightness of the room light woke him. Jim rolled onto his side, just as he had every morning for the past four months. He lowered his pajama bottom and waited for the attendant. Jim fought the sensuousness that stormed him as a thermometer was inserted into his rectum, then lay quietly as the Jamaican took his pulse.

Again he fought sensuousness as the thermometer was removed and was rewarded with a feeling of revulsion.

"Damn you," he said.

"Heard you are leaving today."

"You get off sticking thermometers up asses?"

"It's like I told you before Mr. Martin, if I stick it in a patient's mouth they bite it in half."

"It's the last time up mine."

"Some come back. Maybe you won't."

"I'm not like other patients."

"Right, none of you are."

"Okay, okay. How am I?" he asked.

"Same as always, normal." The attendant moved to where Paul, his roommate, waited.

Beneath his blanket Jim delicately caressed his own body as he waited for the attendant to leave the room, then spoke to Paul, "Well, that's my last time and I'm still intact. Think you can manage without me."

"I'll be fine," Paul answered.

Jim knew Paul wouldn't be fine. Paul was a loser. Jim got out of bed, removed his pajama top, gathered towel, soap, and toothbrush and walked to the ward bathroom. He'd shave later when the razors were released and while an attendant watched.

He scrutinized his face in the mirror while brushing his teeth.

"What the hell are you smiling about?" he asked himself. "Think old buddy, today's the day we get out of here," he answered.

"You're right, that lousy shrink said I could make the adjustment."

"Some adjustment: boring work, weary sex, dull parties."

"You have Ann."

"Screw off."

"And your mother."

He winked and his reflection leered back at him.

In the dining area he drank prune juice, toyed with his fried eggs and soggy toast and finally stirred four spoons of sugar in his coffee and sipped at it.

"So you're leaving today, Jim." Jim looked up. Across the table he saw lips moving, a tongue rolling. He tried to associate a name to the movements but he couldn't.

"Right, finish breakfast, get dressed, see my shrink and out of here," he mouthed back before taking a bite of egg.

"They tell me I'll be leaving soon."

Jim looked up. Now he recognized the mouth. It was Arnold.

Arnold was a nut. Jim knew Arnold should never get out. The world wouldn't be safe with Arnold out.

"Yeah, sure," Jim said. He gulped his coffee and left.

As he changed into his street clothes he savored the feel of soft wool against his skin. He carefully dimpled his tie and dusted each shoe against the back of his pant legs.

Jim rehearsed the emotions he would display when he talked with his shrink, Knight: gripe a little, tell a joke on himself, show gratitude and act adjusted. That was the ticket out. At 10:35 he walked into Knight's office. He sat down without an invitation and watched Knight light one cigarette from another. Jim pulled a silver cigarette lighter from his jacket pocket and lit a cigarillo. Lighters were a liberty denied most patients. Jim cherished his privilege and smoked because of it. Cigarillos were another status symbol.

Knight looked up and smiled, "Glad to be leaving us, Mr. Martin?"

"Sure, I'm getting damn tired of having a thermometer stuck up my ass every morning."

"Getting tired. Is that the only reason?" Knight pried.

"No, it's just good to be getting out." Jim hoped Knight wouldn't follow this line of questioning. He watched cautiously.

Knight began to frame another question and then paused.

"You make an excellent appearance in those clothes, Mr. Martin."

"Thank you. My mother made the selection for me."

"You've been a good patient. I'm pleased with your progress."

"I've had a good doctor."

"Thanks Jim, I hope you won't be back," Knight relaxed.

"I won't," Jim smiled. The ordeal was over.

He walked down the long corridor to the last locked door, rang the bell, showed his pass to the attendant and stepped through the door into the lobby. His mother stood up, smoothed the skirt of her gray silk suit and moved toward him in her inevitably poised manner.

They embraced. Her tongue brushed against his upper lip and instantly withdrew.

"How are you, Jim?" He inhaled her warm breath, her mouth only inches from his lips.

"Never better. I really missed you," as when he was a small child he wanted to touch her eye, her throat, her hair but knew she would anger if he mussed her make up. He touched her cheek lightly with his lips.

"You look fine. I missed you too," stroking his upper arm.

"I've been leading a clean life. Where's Dad?"

"Your father had a pressing business conference."

"Ann called me yesterday. I thought she was coming too."

"Ann and I thought it best if only one of us came. Naturally that would be me. Ann will be so glad to see you."

"She's all right?"

"She's such a perfect girl. So respectful. She's having dinner with us tonight if you feel up to it."

"That's fine. I always like seeing her."

"She is your fiancee. I'm not sure you fully realize just how lucky you are. You will drive, won't you?"

"Sure, have to get back into the swing of things."

Inside the car he stroked his hands along the smooth roundness of the steering wheel. He paused, took the ignition key from his mother, felt its firmness and slowly inserted it into place. He eased the car into gear, swung it onto the highway and started the drive home. They rode in silence. His mother switched on WKCL, the classics station, then lightly touched his thigh, commanding his attention.

"You've always liked the classics, Jim."

"I never listened to them in the hospital. Just mind deadening television."

"That's all behind you now. Aren't you going a little fast?"

"Sorry, this car is like a woman, formidable and demanding."

"And like a woman you must treat her gently, keep her safe."

He pulled into their driveway and helped his mother from the car. They held hands as they walked to the house. As she removed her hat he noticed the little red veins in her cheek were more pronounced, her wrinkles deeper. Funny, he thought, how people change in four months.

"Is 11:45 too early for a drink?" he asked. "Particularly for a man who hasn't had one for seventeen weeks, two days, and nine hours."

"Of course not. I'll be with you as soon as I have lunch started."

Eight minutes later his mother joined him, again they embraced and he felt the electrifying effect of her body close to his.

He wanted to press her closer, stroke her, giggle, be a little boy again, rub tiny hands on her face, push fingers in her mouth. Play at being her dentist.

She had pushed him away then, rejected his want, "That's dirty. Don't do that."

She would always be aloof from him, touching only on her terms. He thought of Ann, how sometimes she too withdrew from him, rejected his need.

He fixed a vodka martini for his mother and a second one for himself. His mother took a chair facing him. Carefully allowed him to watch as she crossed her legs.

She sipped from her drink, "I love having you back with me, Jim."

"It's good to be back. I was a long way gone."

"Mental illness is like any other illness. If you catch it in time you can cure it."

"I suppose."

"Your father," he could hear the resignation in her voice.

"Hold it a second. I'll get us some scallions and celery to go with these martinis."

When he returned with the vegetables his mother continued, "insists you start work with the firm next week."

"Fine."

"But only for a few weeks. You and Ann should get married next month, not wait any longer. I do so look forward to your getting married, going to Europe."

"I'm glad we're going. Ann's not worried?"

"Of course not. Recovery from the type of illness you had makes you stronger than someone who has never been unadjusted."

"You take it calmly enough."

"Dr. Knight explained it."

"Yeah," he said, "I'm really adjusted now."

He remembered his first insight. Six weeks ago while policing the grounds he stooped to pick up a gum wrapper, cradled it in his hand, opened it, read the brand name, Juicy Fruit. He had asked himself if he were born to smooth and read gum wrappers but knew that he was born for finer acts.

That same evening at a dance for patients he had his second insight. One of the women said to him, "I'm leaving next Monday."

"Going home?"

"No, to Taylorville. They say I need more custodial care and I can get it there."

She tried to smile but her face showed pain. She walked to a corner of the room and wept silently until an attendant led her away. Jim told himself then that he never would be led away.

"Want to mix me another martini Jim?"

"Sure, I'd make a good bartender."

"You'll make a better broker."

He didn't want to be a broker. He thought of going to his father's office, raising a family with Ann, playing golf, listening to her chatter. He didn't want that. He wanted to be different, not part of a mold. He recalled participating, while an undergraduate, in a sit-in for justice. He couldn't remember the issue now but he had liked the feeling of exhilaration that came with the protest.

"Thanks dear," his mother said as he handed her a martini.

Their hands touched. She held his, the even warmth of her hand contrasting against the smooth coolness of the glass. He gripped her hand as he recalled Knight's questions probing painfully into his psyche. When this had failed to get results shock treatment followed. He could see himself breaking from the attendants and running. He didn't want that. He couldn't stand the pain of non-adjustment.

Patiently they pursued him, knowing he couldn't go anywhere. They caught him and strapped him to a table and sent volts of electricity surging through his body. Then with a final flash of insight he knew the answer. He didn't have to adjust with his mind, only his body. He only needed to repeat certain well-defined patterns of doing and saying. Then his body would be adjusted while his mind remained free.

He looked at his mother and wondered if she had realized the same thing long ago. She finished her drink and smiled at him.

"Jim, I need to check on lunch but it will be at least twenty more minutes." She handed him her empty glass and looked expectantly at him. He kissed her mouth, she smiled, turned and walked toward the kitchen, her derriere rocking.

"I'll fix us another drink," he said.

"Oh, and dear be sure to phone Ann. I told her you would call when we got home."

"Right after lunch," he said. "I need to talk to her about the honeymoon."

"Ann already knows I'll be joining you in Greece."

He began mixing drinks.

§ § §

John Hayes of Catonsville, Maryland is a poet, writer, playright, sculptor and photographer with numerous publishing credits. He provided the cover photography for FRIDAY NIGHT DESPERATE (IM Press), available at amazon.com or call 301-587-1202.

FIRST WORLD WAYS

by

Jean Heilprin

My dentist wants to take me out for a drink. My mouth is killing me, though—well, not while my mouth is killing me, she says. I've needed two root canals, and this is our fourth three-hour appointment in a week. Today she made a couple of mistakes, drilling a little too far on the measial-lingual of one tooth, not far enough on the distal surface of the other, afraid she might perforate a canal. "I'm about ready to write you a check and pay for it and let someone else do it," she says.

I laugh. I tell my dentist one difference I've noticed between women students and men students here at the dental school clinic is that the women show it more when they doubt themselves. This is the same old observation, I know, a stereotype even, and I'm saying it mostly to reassure her. I can see she's beginning to regret revealing her nervousness this afternoon, and I'm confident her work is as good as anyone's.

"That's true," she replies gratefully, as if I've said something she has known all along but never thought quite prudent to share. "When the men have a bad day I never know it."

While my mouth has been sealed off under a sheet of rubber stretched over a plastic frame, a rubber dam, my dentist has told me a lot about herself, enough so that what I'd really like to say to her is that I think she ought to leave her husband. He is a doctor in a city a thousand miles away. While she's finishing school, they see each other once or twice a month. The man I'm involved with is an American living abroad. So my dentist and I have found common ground commiserating about the difficulty of resuming an intimacy after it loses its dailiness. Our conversation fits yet another gender stereotype about the kinds of information women exchange with women. There is a lot we might say, but, since we meet only inside a small cubicle in the endodonics department and haven't known each other long, we crack jokes. Although we are frank, we skirt the details. It's not as though I've had much chance to talk, either, lying here with my mouth full of equipment.

She is petite, Korean and trim; I am frizzy-haired, East European, thicker. She strikes me as organized and neat. I make my way through life in cozy dishevelment. We find that we are the same age.

Three decades ago her parents abandoned a printing business in Seoul to emigrate to Seattle. Several years after that her father died in a car accident, leaving his wife with three children under the age of six. The mother managed to earn two degrees and become a psychologist. She still lights candles to her husband's soul every year. The family practiced a combination of Buddhism and Catholicism, but now only the mother is religious. My dentist says she finds the ceremony comforting, so she continues to take part in it with her mother.

I descend from German and Polish-Jewish heretics who came to the United States before the American Civil War. My parents were teachers and writers, and they raised me in the Unitarian Church. I tell my dentist that among my memories of Sunday mornings are nature walks to identify trees on the church grounds, a course in decision-making where we allocated resources among a group of people stranded on the moon, and another about sexualilty, in which eighth graders sat around the perimeter of a room on the floor while our teachers, a married couple, played a recording of Bob Dylan singing "Lay Lady Lay." Once, as my parents and I toured the Beineke Rare Book Library on my first day at Yale, my mother said that if I ever wanted to pray, I should come there.

As far as I'm concerned, my dentist has as good as told me she's no longer in love with him. Her sense of humor is fatalistic, her tone mildly self-mocking.

Now, this session done and a lesser pain from today's drilling piercing through what's left of my novocaine tingle, I realize how preposterous it is of me to even imagine giving her such advice. She's the one who does the traveling so they can be together and she spends those weekends ironing her husband's clothes and cooking extra food to store in his freezer because he's a workaholic and doesn't care about domestic things. His schedule simply precludes traveling, ironing, and cooking on weekends. She has different ideas than I do about what male and female partners ought to contribute in a relationship. So what else is new? It's hardly unusual to question or to complain about one's major commitment.

I observe again how personal dignity creates a kind of necessary moat. I'm struck by this because my dentist and I have spent twelve hours with our faces only inches apart, and her hands in my mouth.

What I end up telling my dentist, before getting out of the chair, is that I'm considering moving to wherever she opens up practice when she leaves here. Bad teeth are my legacy from bulimia, and I know they're going to need a lot of attention in the future. I trust her completely. She is nimble and sensitive, and any mistakes she made were from overcautiousness. She explained everything as meticulously as she worked, twirling a tiny file into my number thirty molar, yanking out a speck of nerve tissue, squirting bleach into each canal through a needle the thickness of a silk thread. With a ruler held to an X-ray, she had gauged the depth of the holes, then inserted progressively broader, rougher files to widen the canals enough to fill them with pieces of pink plastic. In this manner, she told me, even when the nerves inside a tooth die, it's possible to save that tooth's outer structure. Gurgling my words out from under the rubber dam, I had said to her, the same is true of the mind.

My dentist laughed. The plastic she had pressed into my canals was the same material used inside tennis balls. From now on, I would be walking around with the equivalent of shreds of tennis balls poked into me at strategic points to keep me from feeling pain. Similarly, there are memories I've carefully selected out and filled in with blank space. Some of these seem unnecessary to investigate anymore, and I'm happy enough with them all plugged up.

Another young dentist assisted us one afternoon. Between X-rays of my teeth in various stages of repair, when I had to bite down onto little cardboard-covered films placed at specific odd angles inside my mouth, he and I established that we both, at different times, had waited for planes in the Santa Cruz de la Sierra airport in southeastern Bolivia. This was a small place in the tropical lowlands, with an air of chaos, patience and inevitability about it, where I'd half-imagined I might get sick just from sitting on the humid, upholstered cafe chairs a number of things seemed to have spilled into. The only substance I'd felt safe eating or drinking there was a bottled Coke, but I didn't mention this because once, long ago, my first grade teacher had dissolved a tooth overnight by dropping it into Coca-Cola, (to make a lasting impression), and I thought the young dentist might disapprove. The airport had had its share of the abiding, poor children I'd seen too often in Latin America—usually in the big cities, aggressively hawking ball-point pens, small boxes of candy and button-sized roses wrapped in cellophane. Aymara and Quechua-speaking Indians, dressed in woven cottons and round hats they might have worn a century ago, sat or stood in lines by the check-in counters, with their bundles tied in shawls, waiting to board Boeing 727s.

The young dentist said that when he was a teenager, he and his father, also a dentist, had spent a month visiting missionaries from their Iowa church in a Quechua-speaking village on the altiplano, a day's journey by jeep from La Paz. The altiplano is the enormous plain, at an elevation of 13,000 feet, eighty to a hundred miles wide, which stretches north and south through Bolivia for several hundred miles between two snow-covered ranges of the Andes.

I also traveled there, and it had seemed a difficult, beautiful place to me. A place that was hanging onto its past fiercely, either in order to preserve it, or because it had no way of moving forward. Things there seemed to have less than they had of themselves in other places: the air is very thin, there are few trees and fewer roads and sparse, scattered villages of mostly subsistance farmers, Indians living somewhat like their ancestors did, when part of the altiplano belonged to the Inca empire. It is windswept and largely flat, the formidable mountains rise sheerly and dramatically in both the east and west. I didn't stay there long enough to discover what it was that emerged, in positive relief, offset by the thinness, the bleakness, the mutedness of the colors; what about life came into clearer focus. I was sure it was something. I watched the Indian faces watching me without a comment in them that I could be sure I understood.

It had never occurred to me when I visited the altiplano to think about dentists. Had I supposed only people in developed countries developed root canal problems? Yes, the young dentist said, dentists were uncommon there. If a dentist appeared in a town, people from other towns would hear about it and travel to see him.

"My dad extracted a hundred teeth in two days," he said, adding that, after watching for a while, he'd pulled out a couple himself.

He described a meetinghouse, built of wood imported by the missionaries, where he and his father worked. It had a clean, earth floor, a cold water spigot, and electricity from a portable generator. The two Iowans stood a foot taller than most of the Indians, who crowded the yard of the missionaries' compound to wait, then vanished afterward into the spare landscape.

These people had endured hundreds of toothaches without synthetic painkillers. ("If you wait long enough," the young dentist said, "the pain does go away.") They had lined up to have their teeth pulled, a straightforward way to get rid of the pain, while I, from an industrialized country, after dosing myself for a week with ibuprophen, had come to a state-of-the-art endodonics clinic to undergo a complex procedure for preserving my teeth with bits of plastic.

Likewise, I'd figured out a first-world way to screw up my teeth in the first place. By consuming hundreds of times the amount of food I needed to subsist, for a period of years, I'd passed back acid-laced vomitus over the enamel surfaces and gradually destroyed them. On the altiplano, this behavior was beyond imagining.

Jean Heilprin *was born in Washington, D.C. Her fiction has appeared in numerous magazines. She is a recipient of a James Michener Award and a literary grant from the Maryland Arts Council.*

SNOWBOUND

by

Robin Herbst

The day before she was born that winter, the story goes, three feet of snow fell in as many hours. Her father shoveled a long track from the house to the garage once before 8 o'clock and then gave up, watching from the picture window in the kitchen as the tires of his 1959 Ford T-Bird disappeared beneath white drifts.

The sun came out at 10 o'clock and for one hour the world shone, unreal and dazzling, beneath its white eye. Her mother sat in the second floor den, sewing the nursing blouse she would wear after the baby was born. She sipped her tea, looked at her watch, and reached for the scissors to snip a thread.

As she looked out the window and sipped her cold tea she thought the beauty of the world at that moment was close to suffocating. Carefully she tied off her thread. Her breath was shallow and she could feel the tiny relentless pressure of a foot against her ribcage. It scraped, as if it had a torn nail.

Her husband sat in the next room on the bed wearing a cardigan sweater. The shutters were closed against the glare, and he watched the news impatiently. His mind turned quickly, obsessively, around things that didn't involve snow, or beauty, or his pregnant wife sewing in the next room.

He was thinking of his lunch with the mayor and the favor he wanted to ask him. An address, and a break on a downtown construction permit. The permit he knew he could count on. The address belonged to the mayor's niece Hanna. On this matter—oh, he was less sure of himself.

In the next room his wife sewed, slowly hemming by hand the cuffs of the blouse. By 11 o'clock the sun had faded and the sky was the color of ash. Snow began to fall lightly, in large, feathery masses. She called cheerfully from the other room, "Your car's about to disappear." Her voice, higher and clearer during pregnancy, irritated him. He stood up and switched the channel but could find nothing but cartoons and talk shows. He turned off the TV.

The gray surface of the screen soothed his aching eyes. However something else perturbed: a memory both titillating and yet producing a strange knot of shame in his intestines. The mayor—an old friend, a crony—had come to his firm's Christmas party the previous year, bringing with him a niece instead of his wife.

She couldn't have been more than 20. She was taller than her balding uncle and wore a tight black velvet dress, a black ribbon in her long chestnut hair, and black velvet pumps. At least he thought this was how she had been dressed. Generally when he remembered their meeting he saw her face, her mouth, which was full and smooth, the color of port. It looked a little swollen. Her eyes, icy pale and heavy-lidded. Her throat, long and delicate. Her square hands, with the subtle appearance of blue veins beneath almost translucent skin. Her hands were old hands, strong, with short nails, ringless. The hands and face, he thought, should have belonged to two different people.

When he shook one of those hands he thought he could feel her pulse beating and didn't want to release her. She looked startled, a little appalled. Then he broke into a sudden sweat, excused himself after the pleasantries, and disappeared into the bathroom. He was 46; his wife was 40. She was at home, uncomfortably pregnant with their first child, a child they had tried to conceive for more than 12 years. But he wanted to run away from her, wanted to steal this creature—no more than a child herself—from her uncle and fly to Tahiti.

He had managed nothing more than a brief meeting by the window, where they watched the whirling snow melt on the river in the dark, and where he asked if she would like to go somewhere for coffee. He could drive her home afterward. I really shouldn't, she'd said. I'm staying at my uncle's and he's planning on seeing me home. The quaint phrase charmed him. He insisted. We could discuss graduate schools, he said. She finally agreed, and he got the feeling she was interested in him. He wasn't certain how to proceed, but he didn't think beyond having her alone for a few seconds.

Later she sat in his T-Bird patiently, her breath ascending into a halo of cold fog. Her shiny hair disappeared like dark water down the neck of her coat. He wanted to unbutton the coat and taste the skin along her throat. Instead he took her to a shabby downtown diner where he would be sure to see no one he knew. She was aware of his uncertainty, he felt. It may have annoyed her. But she asked bright questions about the graduate programs at various universities. She sat straightbacked like a convent child, with her coat hugging her shoulders, dutiful.

He talked. He overflowed with information, monotonous facts, but didn't look her in the eye. He fidgeted. He looked at his watch, paid the check, and followed her out the door, fussing with his wallet. Once outside, avoiding the yellow light from the street lamp, he pressed her against the brick wall and—instantly he knew—made of a fool of himself. He said, Look, I don't do this sort of thing, but I had to talk to you alone. Then he kissed her with great feeling and shame, wishing he could stop trembling, thinking that as the seducer he should be measured and controlled. He nearly lost everything in surprise as she kissed him back, opening her mouth sweetly. She pulled him into an alley where she fumbled with the fly of his trousers, bit his earlobe so sharply it hurt, then whispered, Let's do it now. This kind of talk overwhelmed him, coming from so young a person. He felt almost too embarrassed to proceed. But he did as she suggested, awkwardly lifting her black dress. He felt like a virgin, undone by a lock of hair curling over an ear.

When he finally "did it," pushing her back against the wall, he shuddered after eight seconds with weeks of volcanic frustration. Afterward she stroked his hair as someone might do in a movie. Then she released him from between her legs and gingerly rubbed the small of her back. She coughed, then said, That was so nice. Perhaps you should take me home now. There it was again, that queer proper note. "Perhaps," like a good English schoolgirl. It drove him crazy. His wife's language was always functional and spare. When he met her for lunch he knew how she would wear her hair and what she would order. This woman-child had no context at all and delivered herself like a bunch of orchids from FTD. She overran him with her humid scent and gestures that seemed borrowed from a public television special on lives of the Edwardians. She was silly. She was intoxicating.

They didn't speak in the car, and he felt too ashamed to ask her not to smoke after watching her roll a thin white cigarette and light it with the jaded economical movements of a student accustomed to arguing politics in smoky cafes with younger and tougher stuff than he.

He dropped her outside her uncle's house. She bent down to look into his window, blew smoke out the side of her beautiful mouth, and said in an odd, gravelly voice, If you want to meet again we should do it soon, before I go back to school, preferably in a room with a bed. Then she was gone. His romantic heart fled with its tail between its legs. He drove home to a dark house where his wife lay in bed, snoring gently, and realized his tuxedo pants were ripped at the fly. Looking at her sleeping back, broad and rocklike and utterly certain of its place in the world, he lost his embryonic feeling of remorse and slid into bed imagining again Hanna's strong white hands around him, guiding him home.

Still it snowed. Minute, icy, dry flakes, certain to pile up. Gathering in masses around hedge and tree like tangible clouds. The air bristled with them.

He dialed the mayor's office and learned that no one but his secretary had made it in that day. "Let him know I called, that I'm home, please, Alice," he whispered, disappointed. He switched on the news again and stared at the screen.

He had tried to call Hanna at her uncle's the day after Christmas. He had arranged for a hotel room on a Tuesday afternoon. Ordered a bouquet of red tulips and two bottles of Dom Perignon, which he disliked but hoped would impress her. The maid said she had gone skiing in Vermont, and planned to return to school after her trip. He tried phoning information in her city but her number at the college was unpublished. He decided to ask the mayor for her address. This was risky. He wasn't sure he wanted to expose the urgency in his voice. His reputation, thus far, was untarnished. He had always dealt with being in the public eye by behaving impeccably when it came to other women, and he much preferred to have the word "obsession" linked with his name only in terms of steel, glass, concrete.

But, but. He needed to reach her.

In the next room his wife sewed.

Beneath the skin of her belly she could feel the elbow again, or a knee, scraping from one hemisphere to the other. Another nail, she thought, a fist or a toe. She imagined the milky stillness and echoing sounds drifting inside to fill the baby's ears.

Drops of tea lay yellow in the bottom of her cup, bitter herbal dregs. She longed for the pungency of coffee. She listened to her husband talking to Alice. She used to think he was having an affair with Alice, but had decided that Alice was happily married and anyway, not the type. "Why don't you take a walk, get some exercise?" she said after she heard him hang up the phone. "I'll be finished when you get back and we can have lunch together." She wasn't surprised when he did not answer.

The previous night he had written Hanna a long, rambling letter, then torn it up. He had written her a short, passionate note. He had put it in an envelope in the breast pocket of his suit jacket, the jacket he had planned to wear to his meeting with the mayor. He had even asked his wife for a stamp, feeling a pleasant trill of guilt. Her body, once attractive to him, now offended. It seemed to belong to itself too thoroughly, or to something monstrously determined to grow and displace him.

He lay back on the bed, not answering, and regarded the long slow crack that ran drunkenly from the doorway to a spot directly above his head, where it fanned out in a spidery sun.

He dozed. Slow liquid waves closed over his body, and he wanted to—but dared not—breathe the water. It was clear blue and sunlit and full of tiny needle-shaped fish, thousands of them swimming as one, shifting about-face on silent command. He looked up to the water's surface and saw Hanna's white body, a smudge of dark hair and white glare of skin, her face smiling, oblivious to him. The sun was reaching down to embrace her. He tried to reach for her but couldn't. Then he saw his wife's full pregnant face smiling down upon him, distorted by the water's lapping movement, her lips slowly forming words for him to read. Go to sleep, the lips said. Breathe deep, it will do you good. He tried desperately not to breathe and to swim free. But his arms and legs were paralyzed by the soft stings of the needlefish, and he could move nothing but his lips and eyelids. He awoke just as his wife blew him a kiss and disappeared into the water, a rotund Nereid followed by a priapic dolphin. Hanna was gone. A puff of smoke on a cloudless horizon.

She looked down now at her sleeping husband, lying slack-jawed, his legs apart. He looked as vulnerable as a baby, emotionless, almost dead. A wave of nausea broke inside her; was it hunger? or seeing him there so soft and shapeless, powerless to stop her from rifling through his drawers, biting his ear, running away. Doing whatever. She felt a little vertiginous thrill, as if staring down at earth from the back of an eagle.

A series of thoughts read themselves to her like electric signage on a marquee: He's tired. He's been working too hard. He needs a vacation. These last few weeks have been hard on him. On and on, with withering exactitude she thought of him as a Poor Thing. She shook out the mohair throw that lay draped over the foot of the bed and laid it uselessly across his knees.

She went to his closet and opened the door slowly. Since her pregnancy had begun to keep her home she had checked his clothes with some regularity for loose or missing buttons, stains to be drycleaned or steamed out, ripped seams. He seemed to appreciate this service and often reported to her on the state of his clothes. Today she regarded the respectable fleet of black, navy, and gray suits for a long moment before touching one. She had noticed something peculiar: the right sleeve of his Harris tweed rested very gently in the pocket, as if it were inhabited by an invisible man. It looked funny, and she chuckled imagining all the jackets nonchalantly conversing with one another and having a smoke while the closet door was closed, then hastily rearranging themselves as empty suits when they heard someone approach to open the door. "Caught you," she murmured, and reached forward to liberate the sleeve from the pocket. Her fingers grazed a sharp edge, and she rummaged inside and withdrew a cream-colored envelope from the pocket. Unsealed. A name written on the back. A first name.

She felt her heart quicken and her breath went high up in her chest. She took out the note, flipped it open. Her hands held it in front of her face much longer than necessary for her to grasp its contents. She folded the note and put it back in the envelope. It went back in the pocket, and so did the sleeve, at its jaunty angle.

She looked down at his smooth face a second time. At the small cleft in his chin which on their wedding night she had licked with her tongue for the first time. It had tasted warm and salty. He hadn't liked it, the impropriety of her tongue. After he had flinched she tried to find some other spot that he would enjoy having her touch in some special, private way, a way that could become theirs alone. He hadn't wanted it. He liked going by the book, with him on top. Departures from their script, which had been established from the time they first took off their clothes in a bedroom together, made him quarrelsome. He liked to be able to predict her movements. Invention on her part was unseemly.

When they were in public he might move out of character abruptly, as if on a personal dare: then he would grab her ass, squeeze her too hard, or touch her breasts openly in a caricature of sexiness. She guessed he wanted others to think he controlled her, not the other way around. His favorite thing to do when they were in their bedroom alone was to stand next to the bed while she lay there in her long nightgown, and take off his clothes, showing his erection. He would push her face into it roughly and reach orgasm it seemed just by looking at the hidden movements behind the blue silk bodice while he shoved himself around in her mouth.

She learned never to take possession of him, even then, but to hold her mouth open passively and do what he wanted her to do. Otherwise it would be several days before he spoke to her in private again. Sometimes he pushed himself into her mouth so deeply she feared she would suffocate. Once when he was doing this the terrifying fact flashed in her head that she had teeth and her head swam and she nearly fainted.

When he woke up it was past noon, the sun was out, and his wife was gone.

Without her sitting in the next room it seemed pointless to remain in the bedroom, so he went downstairs to look for her. She wasn't in the kitchen, and there was no note. He decided she must have taken a walk and expected him to join her when he woke up. He looked at the thermometer glued to the picture window. It read 20 degrees in the bright sun, and there was a wind blowing the most recent fringe of snow in eddies around the base of the blue spruce.

He decided to eat first. He gathered bread, bacon, cheese, pickles, lettuce and tomatoes from the refrigerator. He took out a pan to fry the bacon. The counters were spotless. She had washed up the breakfast dishes before she went out. After he had cooked and drained the bacon and made a thick sandwich of it smeared with the orange cheese and lettuce and tomatoes, he piled the food on a plate and poured himself a glass of milk. His mother had made just such a comforting lunch for him many times even into young manhood. It was pleasant to think that the old rituals were still possible to honor, and he felt a rush of childish warmth as he sat down at the kitchen table, looked out the window, and ate.

Fifteen minutes later, the dishes washed, he decided he would go looking for his wife. He wanted to check on his car anyway, and the wind was dying down. The air might be a bit warmer now, he thought, although the thermometer registered that it wasn't, and the sky was slowly filling again with clouds.

Was he worried? He would say no. She was too solid to have anything wrong with her. She was a small brigantine sailing about on a field of white, and it never occurred to him that she might have slipped and fallen, twisted her ankle. That she might at this moment be in pain, one leg bent back behind her, abdomen upturned toward the sun.

He put on his coat, hat, and black pigskin driving gloves. He looked down as he started to button his coat. Suddenly he thought something horrible. The letter in his jacket pocket. It was unsealed. The jacket was hanging in his closet. What if the unthinkable had happened? The thought of her discovering what to him was the most exquisite and excruciating secret passion made his stomach turn. He ran to the second floor, then faced the closet door as he would his executioner. He opened it slowly, almost expecting to see her standing there, frozen in an attitude of horror. She was not inside. The coat hung there quietly, apparently untouched. Of course, he couldn't be entirely sure she hadn't seen it; he examined the folds of fabric even more carefully, studying them for topographical alterations. Had the sleeve rested like that, in the pocket? Would she have replaced it there? There was no sign of disturbance. He forced himself to calm down, retrieved the letter, shut the door, but this time he put the newly sealed envelope in the locked box inside his top dresser drawer.

He took another look around downstairs—in the den, the powder room, the music room and porch—before buttoning the last buttons of his overcoat and leaving by the kitchen door. He left the door unlocked.

He looked around for tracks in the snow that would indicate her direction, and when he found none besides his own, earlier marks, he walked straight to the trout pond. His feet began to feel cold in his rubber boots. On the way he called her name twice, but the silence hushed him. When he reached the pond he inhaled deeply the cold scentless air. The pond was flat and shiny, a black mirror. A thin skin of ice covered all but the middle, and near the edges a layer of snow dusted the surface. He leaned forward to look into its darkness. The pond was about three feet deep; he could see nothing but a few large mossy stones through the pale veneer. No movement. The fish were wintering over, suspended in sleep, their blood slow as syrup. Scales brittle as glass shards. He saw one large eye staring. He thought the fish was dead; then a bubble drifted lazily to the surface.

He wandered the pond's perimeter carefully, aware of the snow's deceptive covering. His body was beginning to feel the frigid temperature; he moved like an old man. He had a strange sensation of being colorblind. He could see only the black pond, the white snow, the pale gray sky netted with the naked branches of poplars and oaks. Shadows of gray and charcoal moved in the air above him. He looked down at his gloved hands. He was oddly relieved to find the skin showing through the openings in the pigskin pink with cold.

An owl floated above him and disappeared into a cloud of gray-green needles. Behind him, a cedar cone fell suddenly into the snow, startling him, leaving an oblong blue well in the white surface.

He called her name again but there was no reply. He turned to leave but something—a slash of purple, a face coming through the trees—made him hesitate as he shifted his weight, and his legs, slow in the cold, became clumsy. As if heavy with sleep he twisted and fell, clutching at the air, at the powdery snow, the thin stalks of dead grass, the white frosted stones, and he glided slowly underwater, his head slapping back against rock, his wide eyes freezing as the liquid closed over them, and the bruising knifelike water cauterized his nerves so that everything began to seem deliciously numb; he was hot with cold; his hands floated up to clear the lacy veil of ice so that he could see clearly the shape that had moved into view. Two thoughts merged in his mind: that she knew everything as she stood above him, enormous, beautiful. And the baby would be born fatherless.

§ § §

Robin Herbst writes nonfiction for the *New York Times*, and is writing a book on landscape srchitecture for Random House, while working on a novel and collection of short stories from her home in Annapolis, Maryland, where she lives with her two children. She was a runner-up in the ARTSCAPE '97 short story competiion.

Nail Polish

by

Molly Bruce Jacobs

Anna let herself in the front door of her mother's house an hour before the party was to begin. A familiar cool silence greeted her. The air was stiff with anticipation. Her mother would be upstairs now, touching up her eyebrows, primping. Downstairs everything seemed to glow. Clusters of glass animals, fragile ash trays, pots of fragrant gardenias, carefully-placed vases that burst with bunches of lilies—pale orange with fawn-colored markings. Even the dark furniture had a sheen. On the pink linen tablecloth, fresh bottles of scotch and gin stood erect as soldiers.

For weeks, Anna had dreamt up excuses to avoid the cocktail party. But her mother was counting on her. She would have lined up several bachelors: lawyers or stockbrokers with tortoise-shell glasses and pointy noses, country club men who smelled of old money and Baltimore's Green Spring Valley. Anna would have to pretend they amused her—for her mother's sake. "It's what's done," her mother had pointed out on several occasions. She expected Anna, twenty-nine, to have married by now. Privately, Anna felt no such compunction—solitude suited her. Still, a part of her reeled to please her mother.

"You'll be there, of course, won't you?" her mother said over lunch last week as she squinted at the menu. Glasses spoiled her looks, she always said, and contacts were too much trouble. "Come a little early if you can," her mother added. Anna had noticed—not for the first time—how her mother's eyebrows, thin slivers of moons, hardly moved when she spoke.

She'd slip out when all the guests had arrived, she'd decided. After all, she'd done the same as a girl. Her mother had held endless parties—bridge parties, candlelit dinners, coon hunts, cocktails, debutante comings-out. Anna's only job had been to look precious in party dresses, velvet hair ribbons, and patent leather shoes, to pass a tray of shrimp and speak politely to the guests. A sharp look from her mother would be the signal for her to disappear upstairs.

Anna pushed through the swinging door into her mother's kitchen. There, seated at the butcher block table in the center of the kitchen, Mrs. Boston busily poked wooden toothpicks into almond-colored crab balls. For as long as Anna could remember, Mrs. Boston had taken care of the food for her mother's parties. Anna glanced hungrily at the caviar-topped triangles of toast, the chicken livers wrapped in bacon, and the shrimp laid out on heavy china platters.

Mrs. Boston looked up. She wiped her hands on her apron. Her white hair was twisted into a bun on top of her head. A few strands strayed across her forehead. Blue eyes sparkled like coins in her round face. "Gracious, you're lovely tonight!" she said to Anna.

Anna gave her a small smile. Her mother had bought the dress she wore. Its green silk hugged her thighs like wrapping paper. "Where's Mother?"

"Upstairs," Mrs. Boston said, rolling her eyes toward the ceiling. "She's in a lather over this party."

Anna sighed. She suddenly missed her father. He'd had a way with her mother. But he died of a heart attack several years ago in his sleep. Conveniently, he hadn't woken her mother.

"You know how she gets," Mrs. Boston murmured while she smoothed tin foil over the platter of crab balls. "Everything has to be just so."

Anna traced a swirl in the table with a finger. *Everything has to be just so.* She
remembered a story her father told her years ago. Once, six months old, Anna had been crying for hours. Her wails stormed the house like a squall. Unable to silence her, her mother exploded into tears, stamped her feet, and then, without warning, hurled Anna into the air. Anna's father had caught her. Now, just as when she listened to her father tell the story, Anna saw herself tumbling through the air, a china doll, a smile painted red on her face, her eyes frozen wide.

Anna started upstairs. Halfway up, on the landing, a glass vase full of large yellow roses, the petals delicate as butterfly wings, sat on a small table covered with a lace cloth. A splash of late afternoon sun spilled through the window, bathing the yellow blossoms with light. Her mother always ordered masses of flowers from the florist before her parties. Anna had often stood in the driveway just hours before the guests were due and watched men in green tee shirts emerge from their white delivery truck. Then, laden with flowers, each arrangement a meticulous work of art, they trailed behind her mother through the house. She'd order pink and white carnations in country baskets, vases of tiger lilies mixed neatly with ferns, slender iris secured in styrofoam tucked away in shallow dishes, pots of lush greens. She'd show the men where to place the flowers and laugh gaily, as if the party had already begun.

"Anna, is that you? Yoohoo!" Her mother's voice shot through the air, the words crisp. "Come on in, let me see you!"

Anna found her mother standing in the bathroom. White and tidy as a small chapel, it almost gleamed. Water gurgled slowly down the drain in the bathtub. It left behind a bubbly froth. The fragrance of Chanel clung to the air. The floor, a checkerboard of white tiles, was spotless. A pair of small drawings of nudes encased in silver frames hung on the wall. In the middle of the room, Anna's mother blew furiously on her fingernails, still wet with fresh polish.

A bottle of red nail polish, almost full, tilted precariously on the edge of the sink. Her mother wore a short pink slip, cut low about her breasts. Her face was a pale palette, brushed with mauves, the lips reddened, the eyes framed in smudges of shadow. Not a strand of gray visible, the helmet of hair gleamed with the Chocolate Kiss her hairdresser lathered into it each Friday.

"Did I give you that dress?" her mother asked. She squinted at Anna in the doorway. "It looks like silk."

"Yes, Mother," Anna said. "Don't you remember?"

Her mother's lips turned up in a smile. "It's becoming. Shows off your figure," her mother said. After a pause, she went on. "Darling, be an angel, do my toes for me. I don't want to ruin my nails." She waved her fingernails in the air.

Anna quickly glanced at her mother's feet. "Your toes?" They were bare, the nails naked as moons.

Her mother gave her an imploring look.

Anna reached for the polish. "All right."

Her mother sat on the toilet seat, her knees pressed together, her feet side by side on the floor. She held her hands out in front of her like fans and peered at her nails, still glossy.

"Have you met anyone lately?" her mother asked, wiggling her toes.

"Mother, do you have to always ask me that?" Anna said. She could hear the whine in her own voice.

"Don't be so sensitive, darling." A hint of a frown crossed her mother's lips.

Anna shook the polish. The tiny bead inside clinked against the glass bottle in her hand. She took off her shoes and, her dress bunching up to her thighs, sat on the floor cross-legged before her mother. "I'm still seeing David, Mom." A lie. "Remember? The architect?" She'd ended the relationship months ago. The zing she felt for him at first had simply vanished, quietly and without consequence, like a leaf swirling soundlessly to the ground.

Her mother began to gush about the party. "Dottie Chambers said she'd bring her son tonight. He's on the quiet side, but nice enough...works for Mercantile, you know." After a pause, "I hope Garrett and Ellie don't drink too much gin again...oh, that reminds me, do you think Mrs. Boston remembered to fill the silver bucket with ice? And the shrimp...oh, dear, did I tell her to pass them around first?" Another pause. "Did you notice all the flowers, Anna? They always add such a nice touch."

Silent, Anna supported one of her mother's feet in her hand and began to paint the big toenail first. The foot was smooth as feathers, the skin flaccid. Spidery veins protruded along the edge of the foot. The nails were neat but yellowing about the edges, worn with age.

"Careful. Don't spill," her mother said sharply when Anna reached for her mother's other foot. Anna shrank at the whip of words. Just as she had as a child, when her mother lit into her for biting her fingernails ragged. "Repulsive," she'd told Anna.

A spot of red dripped just below the toenail. Anna stared uneasily as the spot trailed into threads down the toe. Her mother rambled on about the flowers she'd bought for the party. As she spoke, she leaned back against the toilet seat and peered into her fingernails as if they were tiny mirrors.

Anna painted another toe and, with her thumbnail, wiped a speck of polish from the cuticle on the toe. Then, slowly, she pressed her thumb into the glistening polish on the big toe. She smeared the polish, marked the toe with her print. She glanced up. But her mother was still examining her fingernails. Anna painted the last toe quickly with two thick coats. When it was smooth as a lick of syrup, she sank her other thumb into it.

Anna stood up."You're all done, Mother," she said, a smile playing about her lips. "Your toes are perfect." She tried to imagine her mother's eyes, wide with bewilderment, when, taking her shoes off at the end of the evening, she would cringe at the smears in her polish, then peer closely at her toes to make sure she'd seen right.

"Thank you, dear." With her toes pointed up, away from the floor, her mother shuffled out of the bathroom.

Whisking a rose from the vase on the landing, Anna streaked downstairs to the living room where her smile turned to laughter, a sound that shattered the silence in the air.

§ § §

Molly Bruce Jacobs *lives in Brooklandville, Maryland with her two sons. She writes fiction and essays. Her work has appeared in numerous publications, including Baltimore Magazine, The Crescent Review, Potpourri, and The Potomac Review. Her book, Small Burials, won the 1998 Artscape award for fiction. She is currently writing a book.*

The Last Time I Saw Richter Jared

by

Elizabeth Mary Larson

"My girlfriend. My girlfriend is a bitch," I was saying to the bus driver, before I realized I knew him. Now how often does that happen? That you know the bus driver, even went to school with him, high school?

It was a Monday night, hot and humid. I was between jobs. I had been drinking all evening, one beer for each week left until football season started. That was a lot of weeks, and I'd had a lot of beer, but I needed something to look forward to; everybody does. My girlfriend, my ex-wife's ex-sister, had gotten tired of chugging Milwaukee's Best with me; she wasn't much of a drinker and quit early. You could say I didn't respect her drinking, and there I was, restless and disappointed. She had ruined my good mood; I knew I wouldn't be able to sleep. I tried to get Maria to help me out, if you know what I'm saying. "Let's go to bed," I said to her, not impolitely. I wasn't telling her, "Let's go to sleep." There's a difference that most women, given half a chance, understand. I rubbed her back to prove I was sensitive to her needs rather than my own, but she wasn't getting my point. Maria, embarrassingly enough, was slurring her words, saying something like "Romeo, hamburgers tonight." She waved me away like somebody holding a starting flag at a stock car race. She clamped her legs together with a vise-like grip, though I knew she couldn't keep this up forever.

"Make me do right, or make me do wrong, I'm your puppet," I sang, holding one fist like a microphone, massaging her stomach with my free hand, trying to entertain her, trying to offer her every opportunity to please me.

"You owe me," I told her.

"Uh huh huh huh," I thought I heard Maria saying into her pillow, followed by something that sounded like "vinegar."

"You bitch!" I yelled. I quit being patient. To hell with sensitivity. Where had it gotten me, ever? I told her, "I'll go downtown. Watch some titties bounce. Good-looking girls, too." I let this implication hang in the air like a basketball teetering on the rim in a slow-motion shot. Just outside the bedroom door Maria's dog, a Yorkshire Terrier named Pickles, yipped hysterically.

"I'll kill you!" I screamed, more to the dog than my girlfriend. I pounded the bed with both fists, faster and faster, reminding myself of Sugar Ray Leonard.

"They're all dykes, Neil," Maria mumbled, barely able to fit her mouth around the words, "and you're too drunk to take the car."

This is how I ended up on the bus that night, the Number 8, going south into Baltimore from Towson. I was struggling with my dollar bill, trying to jam it into the fare box, the dollar and some coins. The driver was watching me without looking at me, sizing me up without saying anything. That's when I said the thing about Maria, and that's when I recognized Richter Jared. The last time I'd seen him he'd been cornered by some friends of mine in the school parking lot, right in front of Marty Becker's Trans Am. He'd held his hands in front of his face, like a girl, while they poked at him with somebody's rusted-out muffler. A car radio was blaring Ted Nugent's "Cat Scratch Fever." My girlfriend at the time, a blonde who wanted to make cheerleading captain but never did, had her arm around my waist. I laughed, I believe, standing at a distance, watching Richter Jared's humiliation while Amy massaged the small of my back.

Years later I remembered this moment in the high-school parking lot. I was living in Catonsville, smoking crack from the top of an empty can of Mello Yello, watching the cigarette ashes flare orange, watching the rock getting smaller and smaller with each toke. I was holding the smoke in, waiting for the little bell in my head to start chirping in its high-pitched way, like that whistle only dogs can hear, and I remembered the muffler, me laughing, and the name Richter Jared repeated itself over and over in my mind like a mantra. I said his name out loud for something like two hours while I huddled on a dusty couch in my apartment and waited for the police.

"Richter Jared," I said to the driver. "Right?"

"Jared Richter," Richter Jared said. He mumbled a greeting. He didn't smile.

"What?" I said. It occurred to me that he had no idea who I was. It occurred to me he knew perfectly well who I was.

"You need to put in ten more cents. Twenty if you want a transfer."

I dropped a quarter into the box, grinned at him, and sat in a handicapped seat. He passed me the transfer, not taking his eyes from the road. I waved the flimsy piece of paper in the air, peering at it for clues. It was almost 11:30. The transfer was only good for two hours, though I didn't plan to have to use it. I'd get a ride back with some dancer, somebody too dumb to know she was giving me a ride back to my girlfriend's place, some girl barely smart enough to pass her driving test and too stupid, probably, to ever get into college.

"You went to high school with me," I said. "In Frederick. Right? You lived over there near the court house."

"No," he said.

The bus was air conditioned, thank God, and a sudden whoosh of air jolted me into action. I leaned forward in my seat. I would wring the truth from Richter. It was just a matter of time.

"Look here," I said, but then I didn't say anything else. I had a half-smoked cigarette tucked behind one ear, and I reached for it, making sure it was still there. I covered my mouth with my right hand, blew into my cupped palm. I'm happy to report my breath was normal.

At first there were only a few other people on the bus, but we picked up another rider every six or seven blocks. Richter spoke pleasantly to each new person. I believe he may have been smiling in a friendly way at the passengers as they boarded the bus. He could have been stalling, or else he just knew more people than I did. If he was trying to provoke me, he was doing a good job.

Richter wore his short sleeves rolled up; I could tell he worked out. I pictured him lifting weights; I pictured him dodging a hail of flying mufflers in some gym. I imagined him helping somebody in a wheelchair aboard the bus, muscles rippling like Brutus "The Barber" Beefcake's when he got the Honky Tonk Man in a headlock. I decided Richter was a thoughtful person, naturally sensitive. Then I saw myself running after the bus, and Richter laughing softly as he pulled into traffic. I made a mental note to write down the bus number, just in case I needed it.

"Have a nice evening," Richter said as each person got off the bus. "Thank you," he said when anybody dropped money into the fare box or showed him a pass. He was courteous all right. It made me angry.

"How long you been driving this rig?" I asked.

"Ten years," Richter said.

"Went to college, did you?" I chortled, my laughter caroming off the bus seats. Richter coughed, turning his head politely into his shoulder, though not, I'm certain, ever taking his eyes off York Road. I wondered if he liked to go over to Hopkins to watch the girls play lacrosse. I wondered if this was something he'd ever like to discuss over a couple of beers.

"Don't you remember me?" I asked.

"No."

"Don't you want to know how I know you?"

"No."

I turned instead to my nearest fellow passenger. "Don't you want to know me?" I said to a woman in a nurse's uniform across the aisle. "Baby, don't you?" She stared at her lap.

"My girlfriend is a bitch," I said again, to the window. It dawned on me that I had to take a leak, though there was no reasonable way to handle this without appearing uncivilized. I thought of my former wife, who had taken great joy in offering up examples of my lack of manners, such as the time I blew my nose into a linen napkin at a well-reviewed restaurant in Little Italy.

I stood up, but it wasn't my stop; we were only at 25th Street. "Stop," I said, but I didn't push the stop signal. I had something I wanted to say to Richter. I leaned toward him, one hand out, my fingers trailing through the air. I could feel my bladder, the call of nature. In response, I tightened my abdominal muscles, pressed my legs together. Just at the back of my eyes I could feel another headache beginning.

"Stand in back of the white line, sir," Richter said. I heard someone snicker, though I don't believe it was the nurse. I shuffled backward, knees locked. I began talking to the back of Richter's head.

"Maria doesn't like some of the things I do. Right? We fight sometimes, but then everybody fights sometimes. Am I right? I go to a bar by myself, and I stay out later than I thought. You get into a conversation. Somebody buys you a beer. It happens. Shit happens. So why should I have to explain everything I do? I don't have room to breathe. A person needs room to breathe. Do you follow me? I'm looking for some space is what it is. Time and space, just a little."

Behind me a man began to mutter uneducated opinions in a low growl, letting off steam at my expense. "The bus. The bus is getting hot. People acting like pit bulls."

Richter popped a piece of gum into his mouth, though that could have been against MTA regulations. I glanced at the bus number again, hoping to memorize it. It's my impression that Richter sighed, deliberately and loudly. I hoped I was wrong.

"Well, what do you think?" I asked Richter. I stepped forward, holding my breath, gritting my teeth. "She's a bitch, am I right?"

"In back of the line, sir," Richter told me.

Suffice it to say I missed my stop on Fayette on purpose; I made a decision to stay put. Suffice it to say I did not make it to a bathroom in time to ward off the inevitable. And suffice it to say that I was invited to exit the bus just before we got to Howard Street, though it wasn't a nice area, nowhere you'd want to hang around very long. I had no idea what Richter was thinking, and I believe I said so.

In retrospect, his request may have had something to do with my singing "My Maria" to the two remaining passengers; they changed seats to avoid me if I remember the events accurately. My performance wasn't perfect, I'll admit it, but I did manage to hit all the high notes. "She is the sunlight when the skies are gray," I sang. "She treats me so right. Lady, take me away." I was playing air guitar like Eddie Van

Halen, not that he was much of a role model; I'd read an article in People all about his drug problem. I dropped to one knee in the aisle of the bus. Yes, it's true I was probably blocking someone's exit. All in all, however, it's my impression that I was enjoying myself as much as a person can without actually having a drink in hand.

Richter pulled the bus to the curb, though no one had ordered him to stop. He may have set the emergency brake. Maybe not. But it was clear we were no longer moving. I saw him lifting the handset to call whatever number a bus driver calls in an emergency.

"How do you like my shoes, Richter Jared?" I yelled. "The dog threw up on them last week. It's my girlfriend's dog. They both hate me. I am hated, Richter Jared. What do you think of that?"

Richter stood up when he told me to leave. I could see he was a lot taller than he'd been in high school. He had gotten taller than me somehow. It was hard to figure out what had happened. I almost bowed to him, more out of surprise than respect, but I caught myself in time.

It was the way I stood there in the bus, legs apart, hands on my hips, that made me think of my son, how he'd liked to use a hula hoop, his hands covering his ears, his tiny elbows jutting out, his hips rolling from side to side. I could picture it still, like something you see in a movie.

Suddenly I was moving, all arms and legs, moving with a speed I hadn't felt in a long time, surprising myself. I broke a panel of the back door by kicking it karate style, not unlike Bruce Lee, say, or that Jackie Chan. Unfortunately, it was merely plastic; there was no glass to shatter. The panel fell to the floor of the bus with a dull thud. I kicked several seats as well, why not? There were talents I hadn't realized I had.

I glanced down at my hands; one palm was bleeding, but I didn't know how I'd cut myself. I wondered what Bruce Lee would have done next. I stared at my blood, liquid and mysterious, having nothing whatsoever to do with me.

"Look, Daddy," I could hear my boy saying, the first time we saw a cardinal together. We were in the woods, a father-son walk, the only one we ever got to take. I'd had more than one six-pack of Milwaukee's Best that day; I'd lost count. My son's words had floated above us, in the heat, like dandelion seeds, and I'd had some trouble following what he was saying. Even then, before the accident, there'd been the headaches.

"Look, Daddy, a red bird. It looks pink when it flies."

I rubbed my eyes with my knuckles. I breathed with jagged gasps. Then I was sobbing.

Richter seemed willing to wait for me to compose myself, and for that I was grateful. He escorted me off the bus, not impolitely. I'm sure the MTA would have been proud of him.

"Have a nice evening," Richter told the top of my head as I left the bus. He stood in the doorway, jiggling something in one pocket. "I don't expect you'll remember any of this," he said.

I turned toward him, not without difficulty. The sidewalk was buckling and weaving under my feet. "You're wrong," I told him. "I remember everything."

"Then remember this. Don't get back on my bus."

I stared at him, my eyes tearing. "You can't ask me to do that. Not if I pay. Not if I'm a paying customer." I tried, unsuccessfully, to stamp one foot. "I pay your salary," I said. "You have to do what I say." I wiped my eyes with the back of a wrist.

I thought of a restaurant I'd gone to once with my ex-wife, the Woman's Industrial Exchange on Charles Street. All the waitresses had been my grandmother's age. I wondered whether or not I'd enjoy being waited on by an old lady, but I discovered it wasn't hard to like, once I stopped expecting her to act like a coed. My wife and I were there to discuss our relationship. What was left of it. I wanted to say something to her about trying to have another baby. It wasn't too late. We might have some luck yet; it was our turn to be lucky. I'd heard you could get over losing one child by having another. I wanted to tell her we could try for a girl this time. Girls are different than boys, no way around it. These were the things I meant to tell my wife. Instead, I smiled at my plate each time I demanded more coffee from our elderly waitress.

"Don't get back on my bus," Richter said again, though to his credit he did not say this rudely. He returned to his seat, jerked the door of the bus shut. I could see him shaking his head as he put the bus in gear.

I couldn't hold a grudge; I waved at him good-naturedly from the sidewalk. "I love you, man," I shouted into the exhaust fumes. Richter hadn't been a bad kid in high school, I thought. I sensed he'd seen some situations. I guessed this was far from the worst. I knew people threw up on the bus, which I hadn't done. Richter was probably counting his blessings.

I sat down, though there was no bench. I'd lost the cigarette behind my ear, but I found a wet, crumpled pack of Virginia Slims, Maria's brand, and my soggy matches in the pocket of my jeans. I thought about holding out my two hands, waiting until they filled up with coins tossed at me from people walking by. Then I would find a payphone, call Maria. "Look," I'd tell her, "you'll never guess who I ran into. On the bus. This guy from my high school, Richter Jared. He was driving the bus, can you picture that? The fucking bus driver. Who drives a bus?"

I started humming a little of "My Maria." "You're not a bitch," I'd tell my girlfriend. Or maybe I wouldn't. Already I was feeling better. A couple of beers, and who knew? Soon I'd be sitting in a bar on Baltimore Street gazing fondly at the crotches of girls who liked it when you bought them drinks, girls who knew how to drink without getting sloppy. Some would even sit with you. There was more to girls, I suddenly realized, than most people thought.

Whatever happened, at least I wasn't driving a bus. It hit me like a ton of bricks; a wave of gratitude washed over me, and I breathed a sigh of relief. "Maria," I sang into the night. "Oh, my Maria."

§ § §

Lyrics from the following songs were used in this story:

"I'm Your Puppet." Words and music by Lindon Oldham and Dan Penn. Fame Publishing Co., Inc., 1965.

"My Maria." Words and music by B.W. Stevenson and Daniel Moore. Duchess Music Corp., 1973/MCA Music, 1973/Prophecy Publishing Inc., 1973.

Elizabeth Mary Larson *has published fiction and poetry in a variety of literary magazines. She has taught Freshman English at Howard University and the University of Maryland, College Park. In 1995 she received an Individual Artist Award in poetry, and in 1997 an Individual Artist Award in fiction, from the Maryland State Arts Council.. In 1996 she won the Artscape Literary Arts Award for the Short Story and is the author of* *Stomp and Other Stories*.

WONDER-FULL

by

Kenneth B. Lourie

I recently had a conversation with a female friend about the "Wonder-bra." She was wearing one and I was, well, curious. I was not so much interested in her motivation as much as I was interested in the fit. I couldn't understand how the laws of nature were being manipulated with such outstanding results.

She didn't explain to me how the bra made her look, or even if it affected her body image. She said the bra was uncomfortable. She also discussed how the bra physically did it's job. It seems there are some loose pads that somehow must be arranged or assembled (I'm not sure which. We only talked. I didn't look and I certainly didn't touch, although I was tempted). These pads moved around and it all felt very awkward, she explained. She couldn't master their strategeic placement to ensure the fabulous uplifting effect that was promised. She was not altogether satisfied.

As I listened to her complaints, it got me thinking. Maybe the manufacturer who's mass-producing these bras is using obsolete technology. Perhaps Reebok, with its "patented instapump" should be the designer. The pump, which uses air pressure to assist the wearer in tightening or loosening the sneaker, offers interesting possibilities. Couldn't this work above the waist too? I mean, what little I know about female anatomy is that it changes on a daily basis. Nothing is forever, so building in flexibility that accomodates both expansion and contraction would be a valuable feature.

If designers can create a product that adjusts to the changing feel of a foot in a sneaker, it seem logical to extend the technology to the female breast, which one could certainly say has far greater concern and influence among the masses than the foot.

Theoretically, pockets of air placed in appropriate places could offer a more rewarding and comfortable experience. No more odd-shaped material bunching up, no more imbalance and no more constant arranging for maximum eye-popping effect. Nope! Just press your carefully located button and pump in a few more inches. Now, so long as there's a locking mechanism to prevent unexpected deflation, this enhancement could revolutionize the undergarment business. And not just for women either.

What about men's briefs? Could a more stimulating design be possible? Who among us wouldn't prefer a more noticeable look? This would allow men to make a statement with something other than their mouths (which according to most women would be a vast improvement). Not so much that the protuding bulges would change one's personality, but if it's good for the goose, it's certainly good for the gander.

The brief-pump could use a sleeve to wrap around a certain appendage and provide a similar investment in ones future. Finally, a man could highlight a part of his anatomy rarely seen in public, let alone advertized. He could then bring the body enhancement business onto a level playing field.

Currently, women have most of the items which make statements about desire, sex appeal and fitness. Men, I think, look at women more than the reverse. Perhaps it's time for a change. If women feel there's a place for a product that lifts, separates and draws attention, maybe men would too. The brief-pump will give men the confidence to walk quietly, yet appear to carry a big stick. And if artificial means must be utilized, so be it. I just want a fair shot.

§ § §

Kenneth B. Lourie of Burtonsville, Maryland is a weekly humour columnist for the Potomac Almanac in Maryland, and the McLean Connection in Virginia.

Star in Black Circles

by

John Norman McLean

The Insurance Man sighs. He drains the last of his Sprite and takes a long gaze down the Loudoun Street Mall. Bodies sachet slowly on the cobbled pavement of this pedestrian-only strip of shops. The Insurance Man sits on the handrail of the old wooden bench outside his office. He checks his digital watch and allows himself another four minutes of time off. He tosses the empty soda can into the steel mesh trash-basket six feet away.

The Insurance Man takes out his white linen hanky and wipes off the dew above his lip this August afternoon. He feels the sun on his forehead, each year a teeny bit more showing. A couple of old bums stroll by and one brings two grubby fingers up to the dirty old brow of his olive porkpie hat in salute. He's met by a solemn nod in return as the Insurance Man loosens his tie and half-twists his neck, pink turning red, against his starched collar.

A hot wind blasts down the alley by the courts building as the historic church bell rings to signify 3 o'clock. The Insurance Man gets up slowly and feels tired. It's not even the seventh, and it's been a good month already. Had a good morning on the phone. *Activity. That's the key to success,* his uncle always told him from the day he arrived in Virginia to learn the business.

He gets a little winded, shuffling up the steps toward his office, hitching up his stiff new khakis. *A hundred ninety*, he tells himself; he's hovered there a while now, kicking himself for not getting to that new community gym down at Sherando High whenever time allows. *Heck, it's been open over a year, now. Heard it's open at six-thirty some mornings. That wouldn't interfere with the schedule. Got to get motivated. Got to keep the weight under two hundred. Can't break The Deuce*, he repeats to himself. He opens the door to his phone ringing.

"Yo, white man. Frostbite League sign-up!" It's Spider Jones on the line, player-coach of their Two-State (*the*

Virginias) Softball League team. "We' gon' go all the way!" Spider shouts cheerily.

"I'll be on the hill," the Insurance Man chuckles. He waits a moment and then says, "So the Mick finally passed."

"Mantle? Aw, man," says Spider. "Muff drank more than any three men I knew."

"Yeah, now the media's making out like it's some great deal he made peace with himself and acknowledged his drinking was so wrong and all. TV stations are all full of it."

"Yeah, I guess. 'S like O.J. I mean, you and me would be *under* the jail right now. But it's the focus of every station. Man a'ready got away with beatin' the tar out his ol' lady."

"You said it." The Insurance Man looks out his window on the mall and cradling the phone in the crook of his neck and shoulder, pulls up the blind a little further.

"Got the knuckler working, Boss?" Spider inquires.

"Yes sir, practicing in the garage," the Insurance Man admits wholeheartedly, not embarrassed to be the pitcher in a slow-pitch league, tucked away in the Northwest corner of Virginia. The two men continue chit-chatting about the pennant races and how well the Indians are doing. Exciting year this year, the first with the wild card since the strike canned the World Series in '94. The Insurance Man doodles with the pen he was awarded six years ago by the Company. Through the hole of a sheet of notebook paper, he makes a microscopic pentagram on a Company blotter, repeatedly whirling the pen inside the hole like using a stencil.

"Just makin' my list and checkin' it twice," the Spiderman laughs and then informs him that first practice is in two weeks.

"Merry Christmas," says Insurance Man and the two buddies click off. Ball chat makes The Insurance Man thinks about Skip Elliott. *The Skipper. The turtle who came out his shell.* As a kid in Missouri, Skip was the fat kid who grew six inches the summer before eleventh grade. And the Insurance Man felt just like Captain John Smith discovering The Arm, playing catch that first time on the diamond a week before school, *was it twelve years ago this month? Yeah.* And just weeks later The Insurance Man broke his collarbone falling out Stacey Simmons' window. Riding home from the hospital, he set the plan in motion to make Skip the next great star of St. Louis. This meant a passing of the baton to Skip, from him, the local celebrated pitcher. Young Heat. No-hitters every year in Khoury League. Child prodigy. A regular Bob Feller.

He thinks about Skip at weird times. Like that time he drove down to Harrisonburg on the big estate planning case, year before last. Customer was a retired major league ump. Heard of Skip as the flash in the pan who drank himself out the bigs. Burnout. Another Fidrych. Had heard of the Insurance Man as the man to call about these special advanced insurance matters. Referred by some fellows on the golf course out at the resort in Basye.

"What we're doing, sir, is creating a trust with the policy. You see, the beneficiary is the trust and by law, that trust pulls the funds outside your estate to pay your Federal Estate Taxes. And we do it all for three cents on the dollar. See?" *Piece of cake. Dribbler back to the box, check your grip on the ball. Crowhop. Throw to First. Out. Done deal.*

Right at five, he walks the block and a half down the shaded lane towards the bar. The birds flutter by, leveling off, skipping off the air. That's where the nickname came from. Elliott, his fastball moved so much, it seemed to skip off the air through the dust on those hot afternoons in Florissant, St. Louis, Hazelwood and the various diamonds; Weithaupt Field, St. Ferdinand's Park. Bob Gibson himself said it's physics—there's a density to the air and the seams of the ball skip off it. *Did Gibby say that? Or was it some scientist studying him?*

He grabs the brass handle of the wood and glass door of the corner bar. Twenty feet away, burned-up dehydrated, grimy men pouring concrete, knocking off for the day. *Hope they might come in and hoist a few. Wouldn't feel like such a yuppie bar then.* Takes a seat at the bar, signals the barkeep and orders a tall draft. It's the start of happy hour. Fifty cents a pop. He's two-thirds finished quickly.

The Insurance Man reminisces about the October after his senior year in high school, 1985, and the disappointing miscall in Game Six that cost the Cardinals the World Series. The Show-Me Series. The I-70 games. And how much he wished he'd been with Skip then, instead of in college among non-committal buddies into scoping hair-sprayed, perfumed fun girls strolling about aloofly in the local watering hole. How upset he was at the Newsweek—or was it Time?—article slagging the Cards as something less than a team, because they relied on sinker-ball pitchers, the artificial turf, magnetic fielders and the hit-and-run to win and nobody threw 102 or knocked the ball into Clayton.

Shoot. Just missed the ten year reunion. Too busy, man. Couldn't get away, he convinces himself. Man, he feels out of shape, incidentally, compared to High School. Gleaming out of yearbook pages in team photos, sitting cross-legged on the floor of the gym in standards and stirrups, spikes lined up under the benches back in the locker room.

After his second brew, the Insurance Man makes a circle with his index finger to the bartender for the tab. *Got to see the man out past Columbia Furnace at seven. Way out Forty-two off the Woodstock exit almost to the West Virginia line. Wonder if he still has the corn still...* bought Whole Life from the company years ago, joking about revenuers last time they talked, like something out of Snuffy Smith. Now, according to the computer printouts, he's got three or four hundred a year in dividends he could use towards new insurance. Told the Insurance Man—forget about that—he needs to set that damn thirty year old son of his down to listen to some common sense talk about life insurance and mutual funds.

Outside on the mall, young people are gathered at the three outdoor cafes, munching on nachos and potato skins and laughing among their private stories and jokes, wrapped around with Ace of Base and Bush and Live, quietly, like Muzak emanating from the little speakers above the entrance to the bar he's just exited. As "Scream" by the Jacksons comes on, he feels suddenly old—too young to feel so old—and glances back across the common at the good old boys locking up the hardware joint.

He skips a step over a storm drain and remembers pounding his glove, standing off first base, cheering on Skip in his no-hitter that first year. God, they were like children. And the catch of that lazy pop he'd made for Skip over his shoulder down the line behind first. Rejoicing in the moment too soon as the boy from Sacred Heart tagged at third and scored ahead of his then-rushed throw. You could kick yourself and say man oh man ... yeah, it was still a no-no but not a shutout in the paper the next day, 7-1. And how much that fragile shoulder hurt when he fell on it, his eyes hardly believing the path of the white ball ending in the web of his mitt.

He heads for his year-old Ford wagon. The sweet blurry impressionist image of the only girl he ever loved suddenly appears as a lady with her two little kids scurry across the street to the Revco. Francie, she was twenty-two and had just graduated Penn State the summer he turned twenty, having just left University of Missouri and moved to Winchester. Her family had lived in Winchester since 1919. *Year of the Black Sox.* She stayed at home a year and they were so close so quickly. And all the promises turned into dust when she went off to grad school in Kansas fifteen months later. Francie married within the year. He'd seen the announcement in the Winchester Star and accepted it coldly.

But still the dust hung in the air. Memories of their times together clouded his mind like smoke off the basepaths in one of those 25 to 15 games the softball league fostered. So it's been seven years since his heartfelt words had last caressed her pretty face up close. Tragically, he'd seen her last Christmas from a distance at the spacious Apple Valley mall. She was with two little kids, one was like five or so and one in a stroller. She was standing in line at the steakery and he was sipping the house blend coffee of the day he'd just picked up at Starbucks, having heard an in-depth conversation about how cool Seattle must be by the late-teenish girl with the magenta and pitch-black butch cut, tongue stud and multiple dolphin accessories.

A feeling of Christmas past haunted him, about standing in the flurries with Francie, a feeling of importance shining like the Star of Bethlehem through the circles of blackness surrounding the haloes of street lamps in ancient Winchester. He'd thought: *You know, I'm invisible, particularly in my stupid 10W40-printed Cardinals cap over my unwashed hair, hiding inside this thirty, thirty-five extra pounds. I could walk right past her and she wouldn't even recognize me.* Instead, from behind a tall bush he watched Francie stroll by. Checking out her backside round and shifting, the lost girl flashing her bangs out of her eyes with a conscious twitch, the tan sweater both complimenting and insulting her curves and bulges; the shape he said he'd always love no matter what. *And Heaven and nature sing*, the Muzak played on...

He arrives home and lays down for his daily fifteen minute nap. He falls into sleep and the dream recurs. They're in Busch Stadium and he's coaching the St. Louis team in the '85 World Series. He's standing in the dugout and Skip's got the no-hitter rolling. But the Insurance Man is wearing his business suit. The dark pinstriped job with the double-breasted blazer he saves for funerals and consultations with lawyers and CPAs. Not wearing the uni with those famous two birds balanced on the bat. It's the ninth inning, last bat for the Royals. And he's waiting for the pitch that never comes because he wakes up.

He drives out to the appointment. Ends up placing the guy into a universal life plan and setting up fifty a month to come out his checking into some funds. Yeah, the old guy's got the still working. The Insurance Man takes a jug of corn squeezin's for a tenner. Shares a sample with the old man, mixed with ginger ale. It's hot and awesome going down the hatch. "Clear your problems right out," sniggers the old saw.

The Insurance Man pulls into his drive, humming along with Mary Chapin Carpenter's "Stones in the Road." Crashing through his concert is the figure of a man knocking on his door. It's Skip! A line-drive of childlike joy hits him full force. The Insurance Man looks at him and marvels. *My man*, he thinks, *how long has it been*? They shake hands like the start of the All-Star Game and before he can ask *what're you doing here*? Skip says:

"Man, I'm bummed out. I finally want to take you up on your offer. I am just screwed up." So they decide to sit down and talk. They take off to the old town mall towards Sheridan's Retreat, a mostly-locals place featuring open mic nights and folk performers.

As they enter, a tall gaunt fellow about thirty-five is finishing up the whole-bar sing-along to "Margaritaville," his grin fluorescent through his wildly matted sandy beard.

The Insurance Man asks what's your poison to which Skip replies "life." They both half-snort outwards and Skip's long-lost buddy orders two shots of Royal Crown and two whatever's on tap. *Last day of the season. Tough one for the Redbirds, finishing up a couple games under five hundred. But Skip's showed up in relief*, he thinks. *Ducks on the pond. Bottom nine. Wrigley Field. And he strikes out the Hawk. Cards end the season on a high note.*

"Man, I really need to get my life together. I caught the bus into Front Royal today. Guess I shoulda called. But I got enough for a motel in case you're all booked."

"Negative. Ain't nothing special happenin.'." He is so psyched to be with his friend. And it's only a Tuesday, so this week could be a blast. Mentally rearranging his calendar to keep himself off the road on business. *Hey, we can always push things off. After all, my main man's in town.*

"My old lady cruised. We were shackin' up a few years. Yeah, I had a job all lined up then I never showed. Man. Sold all my junk. You know what I'm worth? Eight hundred bucks in travelers checks. What's that, like thirty bucks for every year I've been alive?" Seems like tears are jumping all through the voice, taking little leads off first but not making a break this early in the count.

"I don't know. I mean I keep making plans then making excuses, then making plans, then making excuses. I mean, until yesterday I hadn't even had anything to drink in like ten days."

"Ya know the Mick's dead," Insurance Man says casually, leaning over in competition with the singer's touching rendition of "Play with Fire."

"Just what I needed to hear," he says, maybe a bit too loudly, although the singer smiles smugly. Skip pushes his half full beer over to the Insurance Man. "Maybe I don't need it. Maybe I'm too tired," he says, crestfallen, bowing his head dejectedly and running his hand over his brow to pull back his hair.

"Whatever," the Insurance Man says in the best voice he knows how. He stands up. He really needs to get some fresh air. He settles the check and they waltz out into the still August night. As they are rounding the corner, a miniature crowd at a church half a block down gets Skip's attention. He says hang on and they wander over.

"Wonder what's up?" queries Skip.

"AA Meeting," says the Insurance Man.

"How you know?" turns back Skip, to which his friend shrugs and says "ask."

Skip rubs an index finger below his half-opened mouth and looks back at his compadre. With a head jerk, he leads the two of them inside.

The Insurance Man has been here before. But it's been over five years. *Made me want to drink more*, he tells himself, feeling his guts tighten. Who does he see but Kevin Jones, Spider's brother, from the softball league.

"Hey, my brother; glad to see you. Need some more help?"

"No, Dr. K.J., but my friend here seems to want some."

"Smells like you could join in."

"Hey, I tol' you" the Insurance Man says rather loudly. "Total sobriety was never my goal." Kevin says absolutely nothing but does shake the hand of the former star-to-be.

They seat themselves and the Insurance Man looks up at the ring of windows around the top of the church room. They could be those circled openings around the top of Busch Stadium. Childrens' art hangs on the walls and he turns them into National League team emblems, all along the outfield wall. Deep cavernous gaps in that outfield, before they moved all the fences in and played ring around the rosies. He closes his eyes.

Skip, you're in trouble. George Brett is up. It's the top of the ninth and Otis is scampering off second. Keep the ball down, Skip. Just like coach said. Let the turf be your friend. You've got the Wizard and the Golden Boy creating their super-vacuum in the middle of the diamond. See,Tommy Herr pats his glove, the cool but humid October breeze blowing back the locks dangling from the back of his cap. Hometown favorites. Game's on...C'mon, Skipper, hum babe. Just chill down, now. Keep it low. Keep your voice down.

"Hi, my name's Skip and I'm an alcoholic."

"Hi, Skip," the assembled respond in unison.

Come, babe, they're gonna knock you out the park, hoss. Hum babe. Shoot it, now Skipper, what d'ya say, now, boss.

"I think I drink because I'm confused. Drinking helped but I don't think it does now."

This won't help you, Skip. You're gonna blow that giant lead. Look, single brings him around. C'mon, Skip Babe. I let the man score on the sacrifice, buddy. That's all they got. Seven to one. Pitch and catch. You da man. Hum now.

"Drinking usually makes me feel good. But nothing's making me feel good, lately."

Don't do this, man. You're gonna drop out the majors and I'm not gonna finish at Mizzou. I'm gonna stop showing up for practice. Gonna piss off my old man and steal second, third and home all the way out to Virginia and my uncle's office. His health is failing, you know. I mean I could take it all over. Do good at it if I set my mind to it.

Ball Three. C'mon, Skipper, now. Laser beams, hoss. Shoot 'em now Skip, babe. Ya walked 'im, Skip. Hold on. Hold it. It's the Mick. The Young Mick. Playing for K.C.? What kind of dream is this?

"I got worried. I drank because I was mad and then I was mad because I was drinking."

That's a long one, way back, going, going...oh, it's just foul! Jack Buck is giving the play-by-play of your success and failure, my man. If I was only sixteen right now and hadn't broken my collarbone. If I hadn't been so crazy just to drown in those long slow kisses Stacey stored up below her giant gorgeous eyes. You wouldn't have had a shot, Skip. You wouldn't even BE HERE.

"It's okay to be mad," Kevin is saying calmly as the Insurance Man opens his eyes. He's right behind home plate now, looking out the black portholes past the cheap seats way up the Mississippi to where it meets the Missouri behind their old subdivision. There's a solitary star visible. He's focusing on that like an eternal pop-up, hanging in the lights.

"I just feel like I'm a prisoner in some kind of prison I keep creating."

"Just like O.J." Kevin jokes to the nervous pent-up burst of laughter of all.

The Insurance Man is gazing out as the very tip of the moon rises up into the black night beyond, thinking about that policyholder out Route 42, wondering what he's going to do with all that moonshine now.

§ § §

John Norman McLean *paints portraits of America through fiction and prose poetry. At his home in Frederick County, Virginia, he records original music and makes killer salsa. A column appears at www.monumental.com/major7.*

Sea-Monkeys

by

Rebecca Motil

The fall after he turned four, Ben decided he had to have some sort of an animal. He was at day care when they went around the room and asked who had a pet—the kind of no-win question I always hated when I was in school; if you already have what they're asking about, you don't need to talk about it, and if you don't have it, you just end up feeling bad that you don't. In Benjamin's case, it turned out that all the kids except him had a pet.

"Shakira even has angelfish," he told me, swimming his hands through the air to demonstrate. "Can I get a pet? Hunh?"

"Don't talk with your mouth full," I said by way of an answer, ashamed to tell him no, but the landlord doesn't allow cats or dogs, and I just couldn't afford to buy a fish tank and a stand and all those air tubes. "And don't I have enough trouble feeding the two of us? All I need around here is another mouth!" I threw up my hands and indicated the small, dark kitchen, the Kraft macaroni and cheese we were having for the third time that week, the coming winter months when our gas bill would quadruple even though I kept the thermostat so low that me and Ben had to sleep together to keep warm.

"Please?"

"No. And I don't want to talk about it any more."

His face fell and he kicked the side of the table so that our plates rattled.

"And besides," I said, ignoring the kick, "you're too young to take care of an animal. You know who'd get stuck cleaning the cat litter or walking the dog? Mom. That's who."

"No! Really, I'd take care of it."

I felt bad; I get tired of having to say no-no-no all the time, but I just didn't see how I could agree to this one. "Just shut up, would you."

He's a smart kid; he usually knows when to shut his mouth and leave me alone. "How about when I'm fi—?" he said, then looked at my face and fell silent.

But a couple months later when it was almost Christmas, I thought about it again. I was at Children's Palace with 30 dollars to spend on him and I was getting desperate—all the toys seemed to cost so much. He really wanted a bike, the kind with training wheels, but they were 60 dollars and up; my budget allowed the 30 dollars and that was that. (I'd put aside 10 dollars each month for the last three months, and refused to touch the money, even when one of the Aspen's tires went flat. Instead I'd skipped lunch that week to pay for the repair bill.) After checking every aisle and bin, I settled on a pair of red plastic skis for $4.99 that I thought he'd like, especially if we had snow for Christmas—not a sure thing in central Ohio. I chose a small ball and some candy for his stocking, and a maroon velour bathrobe that I thought would like nice with his dark hair, the only trace his father had left behind. That left me with five dollars.

I was thinking about getting one of those action dolls for boys when I saw a box that depicted smiling brown humanoids with flipper feet and antennae, the females wearing bows and blonde hair, the males bald. **Live Pet Sea-Monkeys**, proclaimed the thick black letters above their heads. ***Absolutely guaranteed to grow***. I picked up a box and read the fine-print. The kit came with a small plastic aquarium, sea-monkey eggs, food, a water purifier, and instructions, all for $3.98. I figured if they didn't grow, maybe he'd learn something anyhow. I added the sea-monkey tank to the other stuff and went to the check-out counter.

On Christmas morning Ben opened his gifts with great excitement. He was happiest about the skis, although the sea-monkeys were his next favorite. We read the directions and found out that we had to purify the water in the aquarium for 24 hours before we could add the eggs, but when I told him they wouldn't hatch otherwise, he agreed to wait. By a stroke of luck, it had snowed the night before—big, white, sugary flakes—so we went outside to try his skis and played in the snow until lunchtime. By then he'd forgotten about the sea-monkey tank, which I'd pushed to the back of the kitchen table; and that afternoon we went to my mom's for dinner and didn't get home until late.

But the next morning he got out of bed while I was still asleep and the first thing I heard was him coming back into the room. "Mom! Guess what? I put both bags in."

"Both bags of what?"

"You know. My sea-monkeys."

"Oh no." I groaned. "You didn't."

"What's the matter?"

"Why didn't you ask me first?"

"You said we could do it today."

"Yeah, but only Package 2. The other package was their food!"

"So?" he said, sticking his chin out. He already hated admitting when he was wrong, a family fault.

"You're only supposed to give them a little pinch of food," I said, holding up my forefinger and thumb closely together to show him. "Go get me the directions."

He ran down the hall to the kitchen, coming back with the instructions. "Feed the baby sea-monkeys twice a week with the measuring spoon provided," I read aloud. "Add one spoonful to the water each time." I looked at Ben, fighting to control a sudden spurt of anger. "You know that little tiny spoon that was in the package? That's how much food they were supposed to get."

He started backing out of the room.

And then I was totally, completely fed-up. "Why didn't you ask me?" I yelled. "Why do you always have to do things your own way?" I slung the instructions at him. He turned to run back to the kitchen. "If they die," I called, getting out of bed and moving to the empty doorway, "if they die from overeating, it's your fault." I stopped and pressed the palms of my hands together tightly, willing myself to stay in the room, not to fly down the hall after him; it's just that no matter what I do or say, there's times when he's too much for me.

The sea-monkeys lived and started growing. While they didn't look anything like the illustration on the package, they did grow to about half an inch long like the kit said. What they looked like was skinny worms with hairs. They used the hairs to swim, lifting their heads and twitching their tails as they darted from one side to the other of the six-inch tall aquarium. The extra food Benjamin had given them sank to the bottom where it grew into green algae. They ate the algae; we didn't have to feed them anything else for the first month.

Benjamin named the boys Peter and the girls Petranella, after a storybook princess. "How can you tell the difference?" I asked.

He shrugged, but a week or so later some of the sea-monkeys developed round balls about two-thirds of the way down their bodies.

"I think the ones with the big tummies are Petranellas," I told him.

"Why?"

"I think they're pregnant."

"You mean they're gonna have babies?" He looked from me back to the tank as a big grin lit up his face. "I'm gonna tell all the kids at day care. Babies." He began jumping from one foot to the other, in that way kids have of feeling happiness with their whole bodies. The kitchen table rattled in time, causing the tank to begin working its way to the table's edge. I moved it to the counter, out of harm's way.

"C'mon in the living room," I said, picking Ben up and shimmying across the bare floors. "If you're real good, I'll teach you how to do the twist." I set him down and turned on the radio. "Your mommy used to be a dancer," I said over my shoulder. "Not a bad one either. When I was in high school, I was the lead dancer in a musical. You know what a musical is?"

No answer. When I turned around Benjamin was back in the kitchen. He was standing at the counter, hands in pockets, his nose just about level with the countertop, staring at the darting sea-monkeys. I figured he was waiting for them to have babies. "They probably won't have them for a while," I said.

"I know," he answered without turning away.

I fiddled with the radio buttons, but I couldn't find any music that would be good to twist to. I thought I'd leave the radio on anyway, until the right song came on. Meanwhile, I sat on the couch and lit up a cigarette, crossing my knees and tapping a finger against my sneaker. The couch was a gift from my mom; when I moved out she bought a new couch and gave me the old one. It's sort of a pinky-beige color with decorative tucks here and there forming a pattern of even lumps. I have a quilt my grandma made draped across the top. It's a crazy quilt—uneven rectangles of pink, brown, and yellow stitched onto a white background. The quilt is my most prized possession; I try to keep it in good condition so that I can pass it on to Ben some day. Because the rectangles are all different sizes, the colors appear to vibrate if you stare at them long enough. I stubbed out my cigarette in the ashtray on the nearby windowsill, then took the quilt and wrapped it around my shoulders for warmth.

The first week of February, the weather turned icy cold. In the night I could hear the plastic sheets on the windows sucking in and out with each gust of wind, as if something large and dark were breathing. I stuck a finger out of the covers to test the air and decided it was too chilly to go to the bathroom; I'd wait until morning. Ben rolled over and shivered, so I pulled up the extra afghan from the foot of the bed, covered us both, and gathered him into my arms. He snuggled blindly against me and I kissed the top of his head before drifting off into an uneasy sleep.

The arm and shoulder under Benjamin developed a cramp that woke me up early. I jumped out of bed, hurried to the bathroom and turned the space heater on low, hoping it wouldn't eat too much electricity that way, then pulled on my bathrobe and went back to my room to get Ben's clothes out of his dresser. He was still asleep. I took his clothes and put them in the bathroom by the heater so that they would warm up while I took my bath.

After I was dressed I went to wake him up, but he wasn't in bed. "Benjamin?" I called.

"In here," he said from the kitchen.

When I went into the kitchen, he was standing at the table barefoot. "Why don't you have your slippers on?" I demanded. "It's cold in here."

He pointed at the sea-monkey tank. "Something's wrong."

I peered through the plastic. The little animals were floating near the top. Now and then a couple gave a sluggish swish of the tail, but most of them were motionless. I knelt by Benjamin and put my head down on the table's cool black formica. "Oh, no. They're dead."

Ben's forehead puckered. "What about the babies? Are they dead too?"

"I guess so. I guess if their mommies are dead, they're dead too."

His small body jerked with a sudden shiver. "Maybe if we warmed them up," he said, "maybe some of them would live."

A fierce, protective anger shook me, lifting the hairs on the back of my arms. I reached out and hugged him, hard. Then I got the heater and brought it into the kitchen, where I placed it on the floor next to the table and turned the temperature dial around as far as it would go. I wanted an explosion of heat. I wanted Columbus and Southern Ohio Electric to see a spike in demand, leading straight to my apartment. I wanted at least one person to notice that me and Ben were here and that we didn't give a damn about their electric bills and the ir gas bills and the price of food and clothes and new bicycles.

The heater hummed on, the neon-orange coils nowhere near powerful enough.

"Go get dressed," I said, struggling to hold my voice steady. "I've got work and you've got day care."

I gave him a little push in the direction of the bathroom, then sat on the couch listening to the heater. I should have been making breakfast, but instead I pulled my knees up to my chest and gathered Grandma's crazy quilt into a tent around my body. When I closed my eyes, I saw the pink, brown, and yellow rectangles dancing across the back of my lids, flitting to and fro, so vibrant they almost seemed alive.

§ § §

Rebecca Motil *of Havre de Grace, Maryland has published fiction, poetry, and essays in various literary magazines. She is currently at work on a novel.*

MARBLE SANDCASTLES

by

Lalita Noronha

On Maryland's eastern shore, half a mile north of Bethany, the Taj Mahal glows in the sunset. And next to it, the Parthenon, Eiffel Tower, the Great Wall of China. All along the beach, constructed by young architects, there are castles with turrets and moats, pinnacles, towers, galleries and porticos.

My daughter and I walk briskly past a Gothic cathedral inlaid with sea weed, sea shells and polished pebbles. She stops to write love notes in the sand. Uses her index finger to burrow like a sand crab. "I love U!" "I luv U!" "I wuv U!"

We sit on a rock in a cafe overlooking the Rhine and sip white wine. The fruity Riesling grape tingles in my mouth, goes down warm.

"Who is the you in 'U'?" I ask her.

She smiles shyly, "It's a secret, Mom. *I'm in love.*"

I count to ten. "Let me guess. Does his name begin with an A?"

She shakes her head, no, vigorously. Her bangs tumble over her eyes, touch the tip of her nose.

"B, then?"

Her bangs bounce back. No, no.

"C? D? E?"

"Nope. Wrong again."

And we run through the alphabet, laughing as she shakes her head, no, to all twenty six. I finish off my wine and hurry behind her down Wilhelmstrasse.

"Hey, how about...."

"I'm-not-tell-ing-you."

She pronounces each syllable with patient deliberation, pushes me into the waves and runs off. My daughter has lived with me for thirteen summers. But, this summer, she only half lives with me. The other half of her lives far away, somewhere on the moon. And she thinks I do not know that she lives there. I know exactly who the "U" is tonight, tomorrow night, and the night after. "U" is whoever the moon says it is tonight. The "U" she loves is the same "U" I loved many moons ago. She returns and we sit on a log as the tide begins to creep in. Inching forward as a millipede, curling around, gently lapping at the sandcastles, washing over them with determined tenderness. Like a mother sponging an infant.

And slowly, the mighty Taj Mahal crumbles; the jade, coral and lapis lazuli studded columns, white galleries streaked with black marble, all tumble into a mosaic of colorful dust. And the sacred fire is burning out in the House of the Vestal Virgins; the priestess buried alive with a loaf of bread and a lamp. And the small underground chamber outside the walls is flooded with water. And the Doric columns in St. Peter's square fall into the Tiber; the Eternal Flame is snuffed at the *Arc de Triomphe*. And everywhere, the castles have turned to huts, the pinnacles and towers to hills. Everywhere, mounds and mounds of sand.

Suddenly, the air fills with heartbreaking sounds. The ocean is weeping. Loudly. The wind shouts back ugly insults it doesn't truly mean. Sea gulls take flight, their wings spread in graceful arches.

She picks up a piece of drift wood and begins to scrape it. The sun is long gone behind the horizon.

"I feel so confused, Mom," she says, after a long, long while. After the umpteenth wave crashes near our feet, erases our footprints.

"No, not confused really." She stops, listens to her fickle heart. "Sad. I'm sad and confused."

I look at her face. Once, snug as Goldilock's, radiant as Cinderella's at the ball, it now bears the yoke of an adolescent princess in search of a prince.

"Sad and confused. Sort of...mmm...sa-fused?" I ask.

She does not answer. Her eyes are fixed across the water.

"I feel the same," I confess. "Sa-fused, and terribly, terribly lone-py."

For a long moment she says nothing. Then a small smile flickers at the corner of her mouth. "Oh, I understand." The smile widens and contracts again. "No, I don't! Where does the hap-(py) part come from?"

I point to a slice of moon over the horizon. "From sitting on the beach with my child and a moon."

"And lonely? Why should *you* be lonely?"

"Why not? I'm not lonely for anyone. Just for...for yesterdays."

I see I make no sense. My yesterdays are too long ago; hers fall right on top of her todays. Compressed into the here and now of youth.

"Well," she announces, suddenly tired of talking about my lonepiness. "Some days I feel so...so...sa-ppy and confu-xious, I get a pain right here in my tummy." She points to a spot in her belly right below her navel. "I'm so...so terribly sa-lon-py-fuse-xious, I just have to cry."

And two emerald saffires glitter in the dark. I put an arm around her thin shoulders. She feels fragile there in the moonlight. Almost brittle. I close my eyes and listen to the ocean. The weeping has stopped. It is arguing now, politely but incessantly. First a loud swoosh, then a gutteral mutter. Someone grumbles under their breath. A low cuss. Then the briefest silence and a reply. A lapping sound that grows louder. Someone explains something very, very patiently. Will someone listen? But, then the first loud swoosh returns roaring. Slam! A clap of watery thunder. A violent smash. Froth spills all over the sand. Bubbles burst into tiny airpockets and disappear. And then, the quiet, soft sounds of indecisive lapping. A whimper. A sob caught midstream. What is it? What *is* it? And now it starts up again. First, a loud...Please, please tell it to stop. Get the police. Someone make the shouting stop. Why, why can't it stop?

"What are you thinking, Mom?"

The voice comes from far away in the distance. There where stars fall out of the sky. Where comets and asteroids collide beyond the Milky Way.

"MO-oomM?!"

Where Orion draws his dangling sword from his belt and lops off the heads of Pollux and Castor, and now the headless Twins hold hands with nothing to tell them apart.

"Mom?" the voice is sharp.

"I'm thinking," I stop. "I'm thinking...."

I look to my left, past the life guard's chair. A little of the Parthenon still stands although the pillars have eroded at the base. Next to it, the court yard in St. Peter's Basilica is filled with crushed shells, but St. Michael still flashes his bejewelled sword up there in the cuppola. And yet..., yet everything is beginning to look like everything else. A big mound of sand. A steep, daunting mountain capped with frothy snow. A Mount Everest! A Mount Everest in the Himalayas!

I kiss the top of her head. Her eyes have been watching me. In them, I see ancient wonders from when the earth began.

"I'm thinking..." I say, "of how Tenzing Norkay and Sir Edmund Hillary must have felt when they reached the top of Mount Everest. Can you see Mount Everest?"

I point to what had once been the leaning tower of Pisa. Her eyes follow my finger tip, hesitate, then light up.

"Of course," she says, "There. Right there!" She points to where I pointed, then peeks under a smile I'm hiding.

"So? Oh! I know *you!* You want to be the sherpa guide Tenzing Norkay! Right?" she grins, gathering up the mischief and tossing it like confetti.

"No. I'm Hillary."

I jump up and sprint with all my might toward Mount Everest.

"Mom," she calls, catching up. "You're so hyper! Such a total, total spas!"

We charge up and down the mountains that once were the Parthenon, the Taj Mahal, the Eiffel Tower. One by one, we climb them all and when we get to the top, we hold hands aloft and shout, "Tenzing and Hillary, Mount Everest," "Tenzing and Hillary, Mount Killimanjaro," "Tenzing and Hillary, Mount Washington," "Tenzing and Hillary, Mount Fuji."

We have run nearly a mile, conquering the world's greatest mountains. And there on top of the mountains, the night air is salty and clean and the water cannot touch our toes. Orion is at peace walking his dogs. Sirius yaps happily at his heels. Suddenly, from atop Mount Mckinley she sees in the distance, an ocean-made lake that the tide, unawares, left behind.

"Why, if it isn't the English Channel," she proclaims, grabbing my arm. "Let's swim to France."

We race several yards and plunge into still waters. Diagonally across, the lighthouse at Fenwick beckons us. She splashes wildly. The sand squelches between her toes, squishy and soft. Plop, plop she jumps, spraying me with plops of wet sand. A frog princess plopping in the English channel in the moonlight. Our shorts are blotched with dripping sand, and we are up past our ankles in slush. And a beige spot of sand sits on her cheek where I left a big sandy kiss, and on my nose where I scratched an insect bite. And all of a sudden I know. I know the answers as surely as we are Tenzing and Hillary.

§ § §

Lalita Noronha of Baltimore, Maryland, is a scientist and writer and teacher. She received a B.S. and M.S. in Botany (Genetics) from the University of Bombay, India, and a Ph.D. in Microbiology/Biochemistry from St. Louis University School of Medicine, St. Louis, Missouri. She presently teaches science at St. Paul's School for Girls in Brooklandville, Maryland.

Her prose and poetry has been published in _The Baltimore Sun_, _Catholic Review_, _Catholic Digest_, _The Christian Science Monitor_, _Pegagus Review_, _Lite Literary_, _Baltimore Literary Review_ and _Crab Orchard Review._ She has also won several Literary Contests in fiction, nonfiction and poetry: Baltimore Writer's Alliance 1995, 1996, 1997; Lite Circle, 1995; and Maryland ARTSCAPE '97 Literary Award for short story. She is author of _Where Monsoons Cry_ and is featured in _A Thousand World's: An anthology of Indian women writers_, ed. Husta and Nellore, 1998.

THE THIRD WATCH

by

Mary Overton

Lydia sat in the closed summer dark of the barn, the gun on her lap. It was a 30-06 that her late daddy had bought mail order, years ago, surplus, from the war before his war. He'd used it to blow away gophers. Roger said it was too much gun, that she could shoot the intruder just as dead with the .22, but Lydia liked the feel of the bigger gun. When Roger knew he wouldn't sway her, he, too, kept the 30-06 for his watch.

Lydia, Roger, and their son-in-law, Charlie, took turns guarding the barn and had taken turns for twenty-eight nights, ever since the second incident in a stable north of them.

Charlie did nine to midnight. They gave him the easiest shift, when the sicko was least likely to show. Charlie had a day job at the power plant. He had two small sons. Susie, their daughter, was pregnant again and scared to be home without him.

Roger took what he figured to be the most dangerous watch, midnight to three. He was a dreamless sleeper, the kind who seemed to pull a switch and change consciousness. Awake, he heard everything. Asleep, he heard nothing. Roger didn't talk much, but they all knew he wanted to be the one who killed the guy. None of them bolted the barn door, hoping to lure the stranger inside.

That left Lydia with the third watch, three to six, the one that suited her best because insomnia woke her early anyway. In Lydia's opinion—she did not tell the men—the third watch was the crucial one. This guy, this monster, was an outsider. He didn't know country people. He didn't know they slept the soundest before midnight and the lightest before dawn. She felt certain he came from the far eastern suburbs where people defined the boundaries of sleep with alarm clocks. Lydia'd never used an alarm clock in her life.

Now she sat alone, in darkness, inhaling the raw, ammonia smells of the barn, listening to familiar predawn noises. Night in the country never got quiet. Things roamed and called. But twenty-eight nights of watch had dulled them all. Nothing had happened at any farm.

Possibly, neighbors said, the horse killer had moved on. Maybe he was a drifter. Certainly, Lydia knew, he was a mad man. He skewered horses in the rectum so they died slowly.

At yesterday's Sunday dinner Susie said, in front of her little boys, "I'd like to shove a pole up his ass," and Charlie added something more explicit.

Roger said nothing.

Lydia commented, without emotion, "He goes against the nature of things. Man like that wants to die."

Roger nodded. "He's begging to get killed."

That set Charlie off on a rant. Even Susie complained his mouth was too foul with the boys there. Only she called it evil.

Tonight Lydia sat the third watch in the dark of the moon. She wondered about the smell of evil. Her late daddy once told her he'd smelled it in the war. He never said how.

Lydia had brought with her a zippered sweatshirt but didn't wear it. Her metabolism burned like a car idle set too high. She could feel heat rising off her bare arms. She was a small, bony woman, dressed in working jeans and a sleeveless, red-checked shirt, the tail out. She sat on a discarded kitchen chair, something made of plastic padding and cheap chrome tubes. Rust chewed on its legs. Lydia shifted her weight when the sharpness of her own bones became too much. She ignored discomfort. She'd had, since childhood, a high tolerance for pain, and, like her late daddy, a way of rising away from what hurt.

Outside, peepers shrilled. A June cold front was moving in. The black wind swished the leaves and the grass not yet knee high. A cat screamed. The barn cats were screwing. Captain stood up then, in his stall. He peed noisily. The rich smell saturated the air.

Five horses and a pony boarded with Lydia. She had given up having a horse of her own after the last one, Trumbull, got colic and died. He'd been too old anyway. And the last batch of kittens were too young when their mother vanished. Yesterday Lydia killed them on a flat stone at the creek.

Lydia ran an oily rag up and down the barrel of the gun. She listened to the cloth rub on metal. It smelled bitter, peppery. The inside of her mouth tasted like old coffee. A mouse whispered along the floor. Lydia listened to sounds underneath the wind. She heard the cloth. She heard birds, restless in their sleep behind the rafters. She heard something outside move through the grass, the sound of grass being crushed. There wasn't grass near the barn for a hundred feet in any direction, only hard packed earth.

Lydia trusted her hearing.

Now the knock-kneed pony stirred. Merrielegs was old and hardy. She whinnied forlornly.

Roger's hounds started baying. Lydia could hear how they threw themselves against the chain link of their run, down by the house, down the road a ways, nearer to Roger, but he wouldn't waken. He slept like a dead man.

Lydia noticed with curious detachment that her heart did not beat more quickly, but that it got louder. Her pulse boomed in her ears, obscuring the tiny sounds to which briefly she had been so sensitive. This annoyed her. The furnace inside her burned.

Lydia released the safety. She dropped the rag.

Sweat dripped from her armpits into the elastic fabric of her bra. Sweat erupted on her back. It soaked the red-checked shirt, sealed her to the shiny plastic back of the chair. The heat roared like a wall of flame. Her heart roared.

Captain came to his door and looked over it. His ears stood perfectly upright and parallel. Trotter, in the next stall, did the same. Lydia saw them because of their blazes, and because her eyes had grown catlike while waiting. Merrielegs was all white, so her face hung like a narrow moon over her door. Then they all appeared in a row, Beaufort and Sandwich and Gloria, at attention, silent.

The cold front kept rushing in. The June wind blew, heavy and green with young leaves. Lydia realized her jaw hurt from the way she clenched it. She opened her mouth widely, forced a yawn. In her head, the blood beat subsided.

She closed her eyes, trying to recapture the delicate sounds beneath the wind. It made her skin prickle. It made the pale hair on her arms turn and point.

Suddenly, her greasy sweat went cold. He stood there, a dim silhouette.

It was like a gust of wind, not a hand, that pulled back the unbarred door. Such a short distance, a small opening. The man stood there, featureless and indistinct. He carried something in his hand.

The dogs barked to the point of madness.

The horses, stupid and trusting, merely looked on.

Lydia inhaled a stink leaking through the air. It came from her own body.

False dawn shrouded the figure in a sour vapor, a fog. He lingered at the door, unable to see her but anticipating, Lydia thought, that she might be there.

Then two monstrous cats leaped into the barn. The cats yowled. Their cries pierced Lydia so that her booming heart nearly burst from the shock. She jerked the butt of the gun against her shoulder. The cats danced on their paws like skaters on an unbearable surface. Other cats joined them, only slightly more dense than the black air. Where had the cats come from? Now a mad party of them careened past the stalls, cats dodging each other, bewitched creatures made to dance.

The intruder's hands went up. In alarm? In greeting? Perhaps he saw her when the gun moved. The horses stamped and snorted. Lydia aimed but there seemed nothing real at which to shoot.

The man's ragged outline dissolved. The cats chased each other out the door, directly through the black hole where he had been.

Roger's dogs stopped baying. The night sounds ceased.

The fog dissipated; the sour vapor faded and was gone.

Early morning song birds began to trill.

Lydia fired the gun anyway, knowing she was too late. Its recoil slammed her and the chair into the barn wall.

§ § §

Mary Overton of Burke, Virginia is author of *The Wine of Astonishment: Stories from La Questa Press*. Her fiction has been published in *Glimmer Train*, *The Potomac Review*, *Wordwrights!* and other magazines. More information is available on her web page at <http://home.att.net/~mob>.

"Our Coal Is Black"

by

Michael Parish

He wondered how many other people in the subway car knew somebody they wanted to kill. All of them, probably. The seven black people in the car were easy. If you were black and lived in America you had to run into at least one person you wanted to kill by age fourteen. These guys were all older than that. The particulars might be different, the facts and circumstances would inevitably be. But the result would be the same. Someone would be on your list.

He looked at the young Italian woman with the braids snaked around her head, right across the car, just out of her teens. She wanted to kill her mother, even money on that. Maybe her former boyfriend or her brother. Or the girl who stole her first boyfriend from her, or her supervisor at work. Or a nun, a hard-ass nun from school days who had made her feel miserable and stupid, and whose death she had prayed for. The Chinese girl with acne probably hated God. But that did no good. God, good, he thought. Me, bad.

He was on his way to kill a Jewish guy. He had a Jewish kind of name, anyway, European. Nothing against Jews. A lot of them were okay people. But a cocksucker was a cocksucker. Jew or white, black or Mexican. In any language, all across space and time.

The subway car jerked and he swung himself into an empty seat. He gazed absentmindedly at the grafitti scrawled on the roof, walls, floor even. He thought about the old bastard that put him on this damn circus train.

In the mail, every day for weeks, months, nothing but returned envelopes, stamped and self-addressed, rejecting his manuscript. The rejection letters, all the same, unsigned. Except one time some stupid wiseacre scribbled, "*The submissions we get are so many that we just can't respond in any human way, any way that recognizes you as a person. And besides this is New York, where everybody is gifted and talented and we all hang out together and that DOES NOT INCLUDE YOU AND YOUR WORK.*"

Nonetheless, he packaged the material and sent it out again, reading it over afterwards and kicking himself when he saw something he wished he had changed. You never knew what might turn somebody off. It was hard to keep track, hard to keep thinking clearly when you went over the same material again and again, tightening, changing focus, changing point of view. Then he got that letter.

"*Your status as a novice writer stands out like two strawberries on a plate of peas,*" the asshole had written him. "*Your novel is unpublishable by anyone in its present form. Hold on to your current job, if you have one, and work hard at it. It represents your best hope. Sincerely, Charles Galperin.*" He shouldn't have written back, he thought, but Jesus, that was the first time someone had the decency to sign his name. Desperation, man, desperation, that's all, and here he was setting me up, scamming me big time.

He slouched in his seat and fingered the ice pick in his jacket pocket. It was an old one. Very old. Like this guy, he thought—not that makes any difference. We're all the same age when we're dead.

The icepick was drop forged steel and the point was not very sharp. Sharp enough, though, he thought. He found it among his grandmother's things in Illinois when he went home to bury her. The handle was four-sided, a dull grey rectangular solid with a blunt end. One face held the company's name and another showed its phone number—MAin 100. From long ago, before he was born. The third side had the street address and the fourth said "Our Coal Is Black, But We Treat You White." The letters stood up from the surface to give you a better grip. He checked the other pocket. The rubber gloves—thin, clear, medical gloves—were still there, tightly tucked. They wouldn't be noticeable when he showed up at the guy's door.

These office buildings downtown were unbelievable. Elevators, but no real security. No desk man, no cameras. This was a very old building, maybe as old as the icepick. He wondered if he could get back the fourteen hundred dollars or if it was just gone and he should forget about it. What a fool he'd been! What a fool. Sure, a trusting person who got scammed, but still a fool. The old guy had promised him a deal, in so many words, needed some front money, he said, and then he sent the manuscript back and kept the money. We'll see how much good that money does him now, he thought. We'll see.

He stepped lightly along the marbled grey linoleum, speckled like a bird's egg. Thick grey paint covered the walls of the corridor, with frosted glass windows along the top of the walls and low wattage, circular, fluorescent lighting. Old fashioned, he thought. Not state of the art. Not advanced and forward looking, like the stuff he wrote, like his book.

He found the door to the back stairs and put the gloves on. Be methodical, he told himself. There's a first time for everything. He knocked on the door, three times, then twice more. He heard a shuffling sound inside. The office door had a frosted glass window protected by a wire frame that looked like the face mask on an NFL lineman. But we're not in a game, he thought. This was hardball, not football. Funny.

Who was it, the old man inside wanted to know. "Postal Service," he said. "Special Delivery." In case anyone might overhear from a neighboring office. He was glad this place was on the third floor. So many things to take into consideration.

He stepped inside the office. "Who are you?" the old man asked. "Where's my package. Make it quick. I'm a busy man."

"Actually, Mr. Galperin, I don't have a package. I'm here about our deal. On my manuscript."

"Who are you? I never met you. I have no deal with you, please leave," the old man said, grabbing him by the elbow and pushing him toward the door. But by then it was too late. He had shut the door behind him.

"Where's Henry?"

"Henry who? There's no Henry here."

"I know. That's why I came. Henry's dead." He stood erect facing the old man, steady, voice even. "You know, Henry, the guy you said would be our in with the publishers. The guy who *wrote* that letter to you saying how sorry he was it wasn't going to work after all. I knew it was you. Same voice as you used in your letters, the ones you signed in your own name. Plus the signatures. They were almost identical. Plus—final plus—I looked Henry up at the library and he died seven years ago. Nice try."

"Very observant," the old man said. "So I used my old partner's name, God rest his soul. It was only me, sharing with myself. I had his stationery. I thought it would make it more interesting for you, more exciting. More hopeful. But the result would have been the same no matter what." Cocky son-of-a-bitch, he thought, the old man's not even sweating, probably thinks he's going to put another one over on me. Not likely. Not face to face.

The old man struck a pose, like some damn Italian butcher explaining away a spoiled sausage, waving his hands in the air like it meant nothing. Nada. Zippo. *Niente*. "Hey, you got something for your money," he said. "You have no complaint. You got an honest evaluation. Who else even wrote you back? How many rejection letters do you have without as much as a signature on them?"

"You're full of shit, Mister. You are just so full of shit your eyes are brown." The man was bargaining with him, trying to bargain, he realized. We're way past bargaining now, he thought. Way past.

It was not a matter of courage, or fear, or even the screaming need to get out of that office before the minute was over and into a better tomorrow. At that point it was just the feel of the handle, the letters digging into his palm and his fingers through the thin glove. Hit the belly, he told himself. Look how he stands—hit the belly. The thrill was there, the one nobody talked about, the one you always knew would be there when you came to kill your first human being. The thrill, and the sick feeling.

The ice pick popped into the man's stomach halfway between his navel and his breastbone and he popped him again with an uppercut motion, driving hard and pushing the old man's head back with his free hand. He jabbed him again and again until it was done, in no time at all. The man slid down the cabinet behind the desk like old skin coming off and lay on the floor, arms appealing to a god of justice whose eyes were blind as ever. Blood oozed along both sides of the body and the dead man's face was waxy grey, bled white, empty eyes looking nowhere.

He thought about how smart he had been not to bring a camera. It would have been too much of a temptation to document with graphic photos. No need for that, he thought, the mark of a good writer was to show, allow the reader to see, and never, never tell.

§ § §

Michael Parish *is a lawyer with the Washington, D.C. firm of Thelen, Reid & Priest. He has published poems in Eve's Rib and Ploughshares and has won poetry awards in a number of competitions.*

The Empress of Alaska

by

Richard Peabody

The last time I heard from Darcy was in '85. I got this card in the mail postmarked Belfield, North Dakota. A picture of a sunset over the Chateau de Mores. On the back she had scribbled—"Saw Young Man's Butte and thought of you. Luv, Darcy. xxxx."

I think sometimes I fell in love with her because she reminded me of Hayley Mills. She was capable of putting a good spin on anything. But memory does play tricks, and sitting now in the Cafe Italia, waiting interminably for dinner and nursing an ice tea, I wondered why she'd called after so long.

Darcy had been the friend of one of my frat brothers. Mitch had waited tables in a restaurant in Annapolis and could have really benefited from Prozac, Lithium, Xanax, Halcion, or perhaps a soft ice cream swirl featuring all four. I'd thought at first they were an item, but Darcy put my fears to rest and assured me that was not and never would be the case.

And so we went out a couple of times. No boy-girl date stuff. Pretty ordinary things really—at least it seemed that way to me at the time.

One of our very first outings was to a shopping mall. A place I've never ever felt comfortable. Too many people on parade. Just like the boardwalk at Ocean City. And Darcy instinctively knew I was uncomfortable and what to do about it.

There was this very expensive women's clothing shop that was done up with a gold and white interior. White rugs, gold paint on the walls. It was hideous and you almost never saw anyone go inside. I never understood what a shop that specialized in chic furs and expensive designer clothes was doing out in the burbs in the first place.

“I've never been in there,” I surprised myself by thinking out loud.

“Well, I think it's time don't you?”

And to my utter astonishment, Darcy hooked an arm around my waist, swiveled, and led me through the glass doors. I didn't know what to do. I froze. I was sure the clerk, a forbidding-looking woman under normal circumstances who reminded me of Bette Davis, was going to just hit a button and call for security.

She rose a little coldly, smiled her condescending best, and asked if she could be of assistance.

“Yes, I think so,” Darcy said. “We're getting married and shopping for presents.”

I was going into shock. Where was that voice dripping with money coming from? Darcy jarred me by shaking my arm still locked in her own.

“What about the white fur ensemble?” Darcy asked breathlessly.

“Umm...fine,” was the best I could do.

There was a pause, a moment of truth when the clerk entertained the possibility that Darcy was bluffing, inspected our Levi's and Chuck Taylor's, and considered whether or not we were in fact a couple of slumming rich kids. The pause was momentary, and then, deciding that we weren't playing a joke on her, she tripped the magical sale circuitry in her head and burst into a flurry of motion. She whisked that fur jacket off the faceless mannequin, and around Darcy, while I fell more than sat into the cushioned chair reserved for the mere males who entered the establishment.

“All right then, if your fiancee will just be seated there...this is the item Madam had in mind I believe.”

And *viola*—Darcy was transformed by the plush white fur into a model, more than that. Her luxurious waist-length brown hair was suddenly aglow. Yes, I know fur is wrong, and I've seen the ads with the hideous steel traps, the waif-like models dragging bloody furs down runways and splashing the audience with blood to protest the slaughter of young seals, foxes, wolves, you name it—but on Darcy at that instant, that white wolf fur looked really, really good. I would have said or done just about anything, so that she could own and wear that jacket. With those azure blue eyes of hers, she looked like the Empress of Alaska and I let out a tremendous sigh.

Darcy laughed. "I like this very much," she said, turning from the triple-mirror, to face me, and back again. "What do you think dear? Do you like it?" She posed with her hands raised to her chin. I was incapable of speech.

The next half hour was a daze. As Darcy tried on in succession a matching lynx wrap and fur hat, a stone-marten scarf, a fox stole, and coats made from seemingly every animal that had been on Noah's Ark. Skin them, sew on a zipper or a few buttons and you had something Darcy could wear. I was beginning to understand how the first cavemen had felt.

Soon the two women were co-conspirators and I really was reduced to the role of audience. I've often thought it's what I do best. Eventually, I became aware that Darcy was telling the clerk (whose name was Missy) all about our upcoming wedding at the Green Briar. How her daddy the admiral and my daddy the congressman were such good friends. How we'd met on the Vineyard but had both grown up in D.C., the number of celebrity guests, etc.

"And where will you honeymoon?"

"My sister went to Cozumel. But I'm a little more adventurous. Isn't that so honey?"

I nodded.

"We're torn between Nepal and the Galapagos."

Missy had noticed that Darcy wore no ring.

"It's really much too gaudy to wear in public. And I've never liked jewelry very much. Well—visible jewelry anyway."

"He's so adorable," Missy laughed, and gave me a wink.

By the time Darcy and Missy were laughing at my so-called extravagance, and Darcy was leading me toward the door promising to call in a week's time, I almost believed the entire scenario myself.

"That was fun," Darcy said, her arms looped through mine, as she led me out from under Missy's mercenary gaze. We were exactly the same height and our hips were almost attatched.

"How did you do that?"

"Do what?"

"Lie like that."

"It was easy."
"But why?"
"Oh relax—you had fun didn't you?"
"I'm not sure."
"Yeah, you almost came when I put that wolf jacket on."

That pissed me off. I pushed her arms away and walked on ahead. I was angry and I didn't really know why. Maybe Darcy was right? And that was a shocker. What was I going to do from now on? And why, if I liked her, did I walk away. Damn.

"Hey, I'm sorry. I didn't mean anything by it."

Darcy had followed me to where I sat on the hood of my beat-up VW Rabbit.

"S'okay," I mumbled.
"You all right?"
"Yeah."

And I actually was for awhile.

Darcy knew I was a virgin. I don't know why I told her, I'd never told anyone. It wasn't something you admitted around the Sigma Chi house. But she didn't have any problem with it which was a big relief.

"You just haven't met the right girl yet," she said in her all-knowing voice. And I wanted desperately to believe she was right. I'd been living a lie and I didn't want to mess everything up with her like I always had with my so-called girlfriends.

Besides, Darcy confessed everything to me—all about Chip, the wild biker guy she'd slept with when she was 13, crazy high school parties in Annapolis, and how she'd actually had breakfast with one guy's parents the morning after and discovered later she still had dried cum in her hair, about her abortion after a fling with a Middie—all of the crazy experiences added into her win or loss columns. She was pretty world-weary for a teenager, and even though I'd just turned twenty, she had lots more mileage than me.

We did a lot of other stuff together. We went to a tractor pull at the Capital Centre and she got loaded and made fun of the Lycra-clad P.G. county babes who risked near death teetering on their 3" heels up and down the narrow concrete steps. That was a sight. But I had to get Darcy out of there before they retaliated. Another time she decided I needed to buy condoms. I'd confessed that it was tough to do with clerks smirking at you. Practically seconds later, Darcy dragged me into a drug store and examined the different kinds of condoms with me standing sheepishly behind her. "What do you think? Lubricated Rough Ryders or Xtra-Strength Ribbed Mustangs?" she asked as loudly as she could. I thought I was going to die of embarrassment. But it worked. She made it more human somehow and buying condoms never bothered me again.

"Don't hang onto these forever," she said, tossing me the bag. "They go bad eventually."

We'd both read Rilke's Letters to A Young Poet, seen Ken Russell's film version of D.H. Lawrence's Women in Love, gone to hear Ram Dass speak, and even made the occasional Newman Center coffeehouse. I guess you could say we both had a spiritual streak, even though she was a lapsed Catholic, and I was Unitarian.

"Do you believe in God?"

She was always asking me questions. But that one was really out of left field. I don't think anybody had ever asked me that one before. To be truthful, I don't think I'd really given it a great deal of thought until she asked, but I answered automatically.

"Yes, I always have."

We were lying on my bed at the frat house. Just talking. Her face was right up in mine.

"Why?"

"I dunno...Something about trees I guess. That people breathe oxygen and give off C02 and trees breathe C02 and give off oxygen just seems too perfect—too planned out."

She cupped my face in her hands.

"You're good, you know."

I didn't know. I still don't.

I guess we were fine as long as we were sort of brother and sisterly but my frat brothers kept pressuring me, wanting to know if I'd nailed her yet. I hated that word. But the pestering, the barrage of eyes, words, and the intimacy, conspired to push me into at least trying. I wasn't dating anyone else and I'd invested a lot of time in Darcy. If she wasn't going to sleep with me I'd have to find someone who would.

She slapped my arm away twice in rapid fire succession when I tried to kiss her.

"No! Don't you make a pass at me."

"I wasn't making a pass," I lied. "If I was making a pass you'd know." That was so lame, I couldn't believe I'd really said it.

Darcy stared back at me, arms across her chest, wearing one of my Sig blue and gold sweatshirts cause she was always chilly. Her body language softened eventually but her eyes never did. I'd ruined the chemistry and everything from then on was different. I'd become just another guy.

I didn't recognize her at first. Darcy had cropped her hair crewcut length. But her smile was the same and devastating when she spotted me seated by the window. We hugged.

"So look at you," she said.

I smiled. What do you say to somebody who meant so much?

"I got your card."

Darcy laughed. "I'm sorry. I'm not much of a letter writer. That's your role."

"I guess."

"It's nice to see you."

"What took so long?"

"I really don't know."

Neither of us ordered wine. I'd been in A.A. for a couple of years. Darcy had stomach problems and was under doctor's orders not to drink. We both ordered pasta. Her spaghetti with tomato sauce looked bland but comfortable. My Ziti shells were the right combination of hot and spicy.

Between bits of Caesar salad and pasta Darcy filled in the years.

"I joined the Unification Church for awhile after I got out to Berkeley. I guess I was a sitting-duck after my sexual history."

"How long were you involved with them?"

"You say that like I was in a relationship or something. I

guess it was in a way—oh well. I did that for a few years, even got married in Reverend Moon's giant wedding ceremony in Madison Square Garden."

"You're married?"

"Not really. My *husband* was a Korean who didn't speak a word of English and needed U.S. citizenship."

"So what happened?"

"I never saw him again after the ceremony."

"What was his name?"

"Kim."

"Are you still a Moonie?"

Darcy made a face.

"I've never stuck with anything for very long—you know that."

I put out a hand to cover hers. But she slipped away and the moment was lost.

"Are you seeing anybody special? Do you have a sweetheart?" she asked.

The term *sweetheart* didn't really apply to the thin, cruel and glamorous southern woman I'd been seeing...But I didn't say anything. I seemed incapable of the easy truths I'd shared in college.

"Her name's Paula and she's from Charleston."

"Do you have a photo?"

I pulled one from my eel-skin wallet. The photo had been taken on our one and only outdoor weekend, a canoe trip at Chadd's Ford, and Paula looked unusually healthy and tan.

"She suits you. But then you bring out the mothering instinct in most women. A Jewish woman's perfect for you."

"And you?" I asked as our check came. "Are you seeing anyone?"

Darcy nodded. "Her name's Darla." She pulled a photo from her Filofax. It was a casual shot of Darcy and a younger black woman. The woman was a good head taller than Darcy, had hair extensions and wore a Seattle Supersonics" T-shirt. They were outside. Anchorage, I guessed.

We strolled to Dupont Circle. She was meeting somebody else for coffee and I was hitting the Metro back to Vienna. I was just deciding that nothing remained of that old magic, when Darcy prodded my shoulder.

"Wait a second. I need something in here."

I followed her into the drug store and wandered slowly down the aisle past the magazines to the prescription counter.

It took a moment before I realized Darcy was standing at the end of the aisle shaking a package of condoms in each hand.

"There are so many more choices," she said. "Which will it be big boy?"

And I laughed like I always do when I slip on the ice and my legs go out from under me.

§ § §

Richard Peabody *was born and raised in the Washington, D.C. area. He is co-editor of the* *Mondo Barbie*, *Mondo Elvis*, *Mondo Marilyn*, *and* *Mondo James Dean* *anthologies. He currently teaches writing at the University of Maryland, the University of Virginia, and John Hopkins University. In June 1995 he became co-owner of Atticus Books and Music at 1508 U Street, N.W. in the district (202-667-8148). His most recent book is* *A Different Beat: Writings By Women of the Beat Generation* *(Serpent's Tail/High Risk).*

BEST FRIENDS

by

Leslie Pietrzyk

After Amy left for Thailand, I started writing letters to her every night after the late news ended. I sat outside where I listened to the slow night noises I'd forgotten: wind rolling along the desert, coyote howls stretching the distance, an owl. I let ice cubes and tonic dilute my gin, and I listened and wrote letters to my daughter.

I didn't send all these letters. Many I kept for myself in a manila folder tucked between my mattress and box spring. There was no one else in my house, no one to hide these letters from. Yet they seemed to want to be hidden.

I never wrote to my son. There was no reason why not, unless it was that things always came easily with him, his birth, his toilet training, his adolescence. Not one thing challenged me. He was a gift.

> Dear Amy:
> This is something I never told you. When you were sixteen, I called the police and reported my car stolen. You and I were fighting--I don't remember what about, that awful boyfriend and the way the house smelled like pot the minute he walked through the door; or was it my drinking again?--and you screamed that you hated me (like I'd heard you say before), but I screamed back that I hated you, too. Your jaw went suddenly slack, still; your eyes widened. You were surprised to learn that a mother might hate a child, even for an instant. We stood in front of the hall mirror, and as I watched your face, I looked beyond it to see my own. I remember thinking, So that's

what a mother who hates her daughter looks like.

The tears dried as you stared at me, and I kept watching my face in the mirror, waiting for it to change, but it didn't. You walked away, too quiet--no stomping, no screaming, no breathing--and you grabbed my car keys off the bookcase where they always were, and you were out the door, no slamming, just a soft click shut. I don't remember hearing the car's engine start, but when I looked out the window, you were gone.

Then I called the police. 'My car's been stolen,' I said, and I gave the license number, the make and model. I was so calm that the woman filing the report asked me twice if I was all right.

That night you still hadn't come home, and I realized I'd reported the tag number of the old station wagon I drove when you and your brother were children, before your dad moved out.

When I called to explain, the police found no record of my report. I was on the phone, and you came through the front door. 'Hi, Mom,' you said, hugging me quickly before walking to your room. 'Are you all right?' the policeman on the phone asked. 'Never mind,' I said.

Something else I never told you. I hated you only that single instant. When I saw what hating you looked like, I knew I could never do it again. I saw what hate is, Amy, and then I knew that though you said you did, you didn't truly hate me, not even one instant, not ever.

I wasn't surprised when Amy told me she was moving to Thailand. What surprised me was that she had already accepted a job, that the school where she'd be teaching was paying for her airplane ticket, that reservations had been made, dates set, that everything was arranged and planned, lined up one-two-three like a flight of stairs.

She told me all these details over dinner at Rosa's Place, her favorite Mexican dive: sticky tables and great tamales, mismatched silverware and handmade tortillas. No liquor license.

"How did all this happen?" I asked her.

"Filling out paperwork," she said. "Just a matter of time."

The waitress brought a second basket of tortilla chips that we hadn't asked for, smiled at us, picked up a napkin off the floor, lingered as if there was something more to say or do, finally was summoned by another table.

"You knew I wouldn't stay here forever," Amy said.

I nodded.

"I've been here all my life," she said.

The way she spoke she found no possibility of contradiction in those two statements.

"Growing up, college, job," she said. "All of it here in Phoenix."

I dabbed one of the chips in the last bit of salsa.

"It's time to go," she said.

The waitress overheard her and scribbled out a final total on the check, ripped it off her pad and placed it upside-down by my elbow. She waited next to the table, smiling, humming with the jukebox, and there was no choice except to pay the bill right then.

As we waited for the waitress to bring back my change, Amy said, "Mom, I'm 24 years old. I should've left a long time ago."

But you didn't, I thought. Your father left, your brother left. I said, "I hear it's real hot in Thailand."

"Guess I'll find out," she said.

"Of course it's hot here in Phoenix," I said.

"There's weather everywhere," she said.

The waitress apologized profusely that my change was in quarters, so I smiled and said I needed them to do my laundry. As Amy and I walked through the parking lot, she said, "Why'd you lie about the quarters?"

"To be nice," I said.

Amy stopped at her car, dug through her purse for keys, didn't look at me when she said, "That's you—always nicest to the people you don't know."

Only a daughter would know to say such a thing, when exactly to say it.

Dear Amy:
It wasn't easy for me. Isn't that how we all begin an apology, by apologizing to ourselves first? I had no idea how to be a wife, how to be a mother. All I knew--maybe all anyone knows?--is that I _didn't_ want what I'd seen. There was noise always around me, people talking, too many relatives wanting to know what I was doing now, was doing next, what I did yesterday. Aunt Joan stopped by to visit, and the first thing she said to me was, 'So, Ginger, I hear you became a woman last week.' You couldn't sneeze without pneumonia setting in. When I got a B on an exam, everyone knew I was flunking out of school and that I'd never be the teacher they expected me to become.

It shouldn't be this easy to leave behind your family. There should be some part of you that doesn't want to go.

Do you know how I saved enough money to take the Greyhound bus out of Detroit? How badly I wanted to leave? I stole tips off tables in restaurants. Tips my dates left, tips other people left. I had a job at the five and dime, but that money was for helping out the family. So how could I dare use that same money to escape?

I hated Detroit, hated being Polish, hated the way my grandmother spoke so slowly in English, so carefully, each word made of glass. The food we ate was slow and heavy, dense, took too many bites to chew. Winter and snow and slush stretched across too many months. We all looked alike; my cousins and I were confused with one another at school and church. That made me feel I'd never get out, knowing that months after I was gone, someone was calling my cousin Theresa 'Ginger.'

But was there one part of me that refused to go, one part wanting to stay behind?

I never thought anyone else would know this about me, but I was crying as the Greyhound bus pulled away from the curb. I was bawling so hard that women looked away instead of handing me tissues from their purses; they were that afraid of my sorrow. I hated that I cried that way, what it meant.

Amy, go back and reread this letter, and X out the paragraph before this one. This is what I thought no one would ever know about me: My mother cried; my grandmother, my aunts, my cousins all cried. Even my father slipped off his glasses and wiped at his eyes with a handkerchief. But when the bus pulled away from the curb, I was still waving my white gloves out the window, calling my promises to write lots of letters, and it wasn't until halfway down the block that I realized I hadn't cried. I remember thinking, now I'm going to cry; I'm going to cry because I should have, and I didn't. The entire bus trip I didn't. Are you surprised?

Are you? You didn't cry at the airport on your way to Thailand. You kissed, hugged, fussed with luggage, waved, bought magazines, ate a sandwich, but you didn't cry. I watched you.

As you watched me. I didn't cry until after your plane was no longer a number on the flight monitor, after I found the airport bar and had a martini (maybe it was two, more likely three, probably four). Not until then.

You learned about leaving from me. What else?

Amy asked, "Do you need a drink to get through the day?" She was reading out of a magazine. I knew exactly what she was getting at. She was fourteen, certain she was sly.

I said, "No."

"Does your drinking affect your job?"

"No."

"Is it why Dad left?"

The magazine was on her lap, and she was looking straight at me. I set down the memos I was reading, pushed them aside.

"No, that's not why Dad left," I said. I opened my briefcase, pretended I was looking for something at the bottom.

"Does your drinking make you lie?" she asked.

The briefcase fell shut. I couldn't tell if she was reading from a magazine article or not, if in fact she'd ever been reading from the magazine. It was still in her lap, still open.

"Are you saying that your mother lies?" I asked.

"Just answer the question please."

"No," I said.

"Is that your answer? Or is that 'no, I won't answer the question?'" She sat up straighter, pushed her hair behind her ears.

"Just no," I said. "What are you reading anyway?"

"None of your business," she said.

"What makes you think these questions are your business?" I asked.

"Dad left because you're a drunk, didn't he?"

I was tired of working a full day and taking two classes at night, tired of trying to hold everything together. There should have been a joke that would get the smirk off her face and the sweat off mine, a joke that could put us together into a hug, a giggle, but hell if I knew any joke that good. I said, "He left because we decided it would be the best thing for both of us."

"Is it the best thing for me?" she asked.

"It's better for all of us," I said.

"I don't believe you," she said.

When did she get too big to send to her room? I said, "Ask your father if you don't believe me."

She said, "I already did."

"So you believe him, not me?" I could sound casual, too, tossing off words like they were nothing.

The bulb in the overhead light suddenly fizzled and popped. Odd shadows off the lamp at my side criss-crossed the wall. Amy flipped her magazine closed. "You don't know what he said, do you?"

I knew exactly what he said. I'd heard it over and over and over. "What did he say?" I asked.

"That you're a stinking, disgusting drunk, and you're always embarrassing everyone by drinking too much wherever you go." The words came out one by one, stacking up until she was sure she had enough.

I stood up. I thought I would walk from the room. I thought I would pick up my papers and my briefcase and go into my bedroom, turn on the radio to soft music, read my memos and then look over my chapter for tomorrow night's class. I thought that's what would happen next.

Instead I left my papers on the table. I walked to where Amy slouched sideways in the overstuffed chair, and I leaned towards her the way you lean when you're about to hug someone.

I slapped her. My hand against her cheek was a quick, hard thwack.

There was silence. I had never hit my daughter.

"I'm sorry," I said.

"No you're not," and she was the one who took her magazine to her bedroom and turned on thumpingly loud music that played on "repeat" all night, even after she was asleep.

I was the one who sat in the room with the burned-out light bulb, watching the level in the gin bottle sink lower and lower until I reached the bottom and then I could cry.

Dear Amy:
What do you miss? Do you miss chips and salsa? Is there a T.V. show you'd like to watch? Have you forgotten the smell of apple pie in the oven on a chilly November day? Is there one type of bird you're used to seeing that isn't there? This is how I think of you now, someone going without. I forget about the new things you're finding in Thailand.

The women I work with talk about their daughters. 'My Anne-Marie and I wear the same size shoe,' one says. Another says, 'Susannah's treating me to lunch today; isn't that sweet?' 'Shelby and her boyfriend and Paul and I went camping together in the White Mountains this weekend--what a blast!' someone else says. When they look at me, I smile. 'Amy and I are best friends,' I tell them. They believe me as easily as I believed them.

It's never the men talking this way about their sons or daughters, or the women talking about their sons. Only the women and the daughters, the mothers and their girls.

I remember the afternoon I found out I was pregnant with you.

I never told you this: Your father and I weren't married yet. Maybe you guessed? I borrowed a friend's wedding ring and went to a doctor on the other side of Phoenix. The wedding ring was too big, and I kept spinning the diamond around and around my finger. 'Positive,' the doctor told me. The room was cold; there was a window air conditioner clacking and dripping water into a pan. The doctor's hands smelled like the soap in the ladies room. He didn't say anything, didn't say 'congratulations' or 'I'm sorry.' Just once he brushed the hair off my face, and I heard the tick of his watch as his hand passed by. It was as if he'd entirely forgotten about the crowd of pregnant women sweating in his waiting room.

The first thing I thought of was not your father or my mother or even me, but you. Tiny you all alone in my uterus, waiting for me to speak. I knew the options. I knew the choices.

My friend who loaned me the ring had said this doctor knew people. He would have helped me. He liked me. There was always a way to find money.

I didn't think: This will be my best friend. I didn't think: She and I will wear the same size shoe. I thought: This is part of me.

The doctor smiled, put his hand on my shoulder, said, 'Congratulations.'

So I became a mother and a wife. Like my mother before me, and her mother and back into the past, and like a long mirror looking into itself, there you were. I knew you'd be beautiful. I knew you'd be smart. I knew you'd be able to tell a joke well. I knew people would like you. I knew one day you'd leave.

Amy, don't think about what you miss. Think about what you have now that you didn't have before. Don't live always fighting against what you don't want; instead fight for what you do want. Of all the times I asked you to believe me, this is the time I mean it the most.

I wanted to tell you this not at the airport, not the day at the Mexican restaurant when you told me you were moving to the other side of the world, but that first day in the doctor's office.

I wrote a letter to Amy every night. I imagined her doing the same, writing a letter to me, except that her night was my day. Or was it my today was her tomorrow? Whichever it was, it never matched exactly right.

§ § §

Leslie Pietrzyk *lives in Alexandria, Virginia. Her fiction has appeared in many journals, including Shenandoah, The Iowa Review, and New England Review. This story "Best Friends" (in somewhat different form) appears in Pears on a Willow Tree (Bard), copyright © 1998 by Leslie Pietrzyk. Permission for this story to appear here has been granted by Avon Books, Inc.*

Nice Fish, Interesting Jewelry

by

Tim Poland

He was a slow learner, always had been. He hadn't learned to ride a bicycle until the age of seven. By the time he learned to swim, other children his age had been leaping from the divingboards into the deep end of the municipal swimming pool for a couple of years. Two attempts had been required before he passed the test for his driver's license. His ex-wife had married another man and now lived in another town on the other side of the Blue Ridge Mountains because he had learned marriage too slowly. So there was no reason why fly fishing should be any different from everything else Benny had taken too long to figure out.

Still, slowly, he did learn. Fewer flies were lost in overhanging branches, water became more legible, he slammed its surface less brutally, and the occasional fish rose to his fly more frequently. But never what other anglers called a *nice fish*, never one of the big ones. And yet, Benny knew he must be on the right track because during the long winter months when the trout ran low and slow and he declined to stand crotch deep in the scrotum-tightening waters of icy mountain streams, he dreamed of trout. If a fish was dreamable, it was worth the trouble, he thought. But there remained a point, something at the core of fly fishing, that he was missing. He knew that. With the early spring hatches coming soon, Benny had returned to the waters of the south fork of the Cherokee River a few weeks ago, ready to renew his struggle. He felt himself inching closer to an understanding.

At a table in the diner where he usually took breakfast on his way to the south fork, sipping his coffee, dribbling more imitation maple syrup over the torn remains of his pancakes, Benny thought about the woman and hoped she would be on the river again today.

—More coffee?

His waitress stood over him, holding a coffee pot half extended toward his cup. Her right ear carried four earrings and her left one was lined with at least eight, from the lobe to the top, all of varying designs. A slight greenish tint suggested itself in her hair.

—Please, Benny said.

Benny knew the additional coffee came at a price, beyond conventional currency. Each extra cup roughly translated into one extra time he would have to slosh out of the stream, lean his rod against a tree, strip off his vest and peel his chest waders down to his calves to relieve himself. At one point he had briefly considered laying in a supply of Depends as a legitimate fishing accessory. But he always had the extra coffee. He liked it, needed it. And like most men, Benny usually found pissing outdoors somehow liberating.

After topping off his cup, the waitress moved on to another table. The faint jingle of her earrings as she turned away yanked Benny's thoughts back to the other woman and her own interesting jewelry. He had noticed it immediately the first time he saw her on the river, which—to his mind—seemed like only yesterday. He remembered the incident clearly. Winter run-off had thinned, the waters ran clear and cold, too cold yet for much activity on top, so Benny had been dead-drifting a flashback pheasant tail. Through his waders and two pair of thermal socks his feet were still cold, and he stumbled his way over the rocky stream bed, lazily walking his line downstream, paying more attention to his numbing toes than to where his line dipped into the current. He counted on the sparkle of his nymph to compensate for his own distraction. Awkwardly ducking under an overhanging branch as he followed his line around a bend, he spotted her, maybe thirty yards ahead, crouching low on the bank behind a downed tree trunk, staring downstream, into a deep pool.

Even from thirty yards, it was unmistakable. Anyone who had ever been in a tackle shop could recognize it. Hanging from her ear, lying against her exposed neck, the distinctive red and white oblong of a Dardevle spoon. From his place upstream, Benny couldn't make out if, to transform the lure into jewelry, she had removed the hooks. He could only assume.

Benny held his position, and so did the woman. She was fixed, focused utterly on a spot in the pool before her. Her hair was long and thick, light brown, pulled through the opening at the back of her ball cap and tied off in a pony-tail that draped down her back, covering half the net hooked to her vest. Her line was reeled in and her rod held still, the tip tilted slightly back from the surface of the stream, the butt resting against her hip. The neoprene of her waders clung tightly, outlining the tautness of her crouching thighs and buttocks. Though she had yet to see him, Benny took quick inventory of what his facial features might be at the moment, making sure he wasn't leering. He had never before encountered a woman fly fishing. He had read the magazines, watched the fishing shows on the sports channel, seen the women's items in his catalogs, and knew that many women were fly fishers. A woman managed his favorite fly shop and frequently provided him with concise answers to his clumsy questions about fly selection and strategy. But he had never met a woman alone on a river. He did not want to appear threatening. He needed to watch her. He ducked back under the overhang and peered at her through the branches, completely forgetting his own line still riding in the current.

Coming out of her crouch but remaining low, her eyes still on the spot in the pool, she crept carefully back upstream. After a retreat of several yards, she wedged her rod under her arm and began to change flies. Deftly, fluidly, with minimal motion, she clipped off the old fly, hooked it to her drying patch, chose a new fly from her fly box, and tied it on. Peeking through the branches upstream, Benny could not make out her selection.

Out of her crouch but still hunched low, she crept into the stream, slowly stripping line from her reel as she moved. Her progress was glacial. Benny guessed she took at least two minutes to traverse about eight or ten feet to the middle of the narrow river. She flowed into the water, graceful and poised, her step never faltering. Her footfalls so controlled and delicate, her advance so slow, she did not disturb the current. Rather, it appeared to adjust to her as a permanent presence. She fit the water.

Reaching mid-stream, she knelt behind a protruding rock at the head of the pool, one knee in, one knee out of the water. The gurgling surface of the river ran just under her hovering, neoprened buttocks, around the rock, and fanned out into the deeper, calmer water. For another full minute she remained frozen in place behind the rock, her gaze fixed on her target, her stripped line loosely looped and dangling from her line hand. Benny's breathing grew shallow and cautious as he followed the precision of her motion and the glint of the lure hanging from her ear.

Her rod tip rose and the stripped line began unraveling from her line hand and feeding along the rod and out over the pool in a series of precise false casts. Branches of hemlock and oak on both riverbanks hung heavy and close over the stream, leaving only a few feet of unobstructed space overhead for a clear casting lane. Her final false cast drifted back. She held the drift for a moment, then snapped her rod forward, the flex of her wrist barely perceptible from Benny's perspective, and shot her line. Her cast rolled out tight and low, elegant, exactly splitting the narrow casting lane. As the line rolled leader and fly out to the end of her cast, she dropped her rod tip, and line and leader floated to the surface, sinking her fly into the feeding lane where the tail of the fanning water dissipated into the deep pool.

Benny realized he had held his breath during her cast. He exhaled long and deep. When he inhaled, her line was struck. From his cover behind the overhang, Benny could hear the splash plainly, could feel the reverberation of the strike that far upstream. In what seemed a single motion, she set the hook, rose from behind the rock, and glided downstream, through the deeper water, toward the bank. Holding her arching rod high and out over the water, tilting the tip from side to side, she played the fish. Her reel hissed as she let out line, letting it run as much as she could in the tight space. Her line hand pulled down in a retrieve, and a glistening, writhing rainbow jumped.

—Jesus. Nice fish, Benny muttered. Must be four or five pounds.

Nearly at the bank now, she continued to let it run, leading it back and forth across the pool, guiding it away from possible snags, wearing it down. Her straining rod high over her head, she began a slow retrieve, carefully reclaiming her taut line from the wearying fish.

Intending to rush downstream and help her net the big rainbow, Benny lurched quickly from his hiding place and slipped on a slick rock in the stream bed. By the time he regained his equilibrium and wiped the water from his face, he sat butt-down, his legs splayed before him, up to his waist in the rushing current of the south fork.

—Damn it, he said.

He looked downstream to see if he had been exposed. If she had seen him, his condition had not warranted much attention. She was kneeling at the water's edge, slipping her net under the big rainbow. From his seat upstream Benny could see the deep, heavy bow of her net and the flapping tail of the fish protruding from it. She had already removed her fly and held the fish down in the current by its tail and belly, resting it, by the time Benny struggled back to his feet and realized that something tugged lightly on the end of his own forgotten line. The tip of his rod barely twitched as he quickly pulled in his fish, a young, six-inch rainbow, as awkward and inexperienced as he. Bending to free his fish, Benny looked downstream at the woman as she sent the big rainbow gliding back into the depths of the pool. By the time Benny had twisted and wiggled his pheasant tail from the little rainbow's mouth, dislodging a chunk of the trout's lip in the process, the woman had disappeared downstream, gone in the streamside brush. He crawled up the bank and peed against a tree.

An hour later, after Benny had tried a half dozen different flies and whipped the calm surface of the deep pool into a boiling froth, driving down every trout in his line's radius, he saw the woman again. She strode the ridge atop the riverbank, her rod resting against her shoulder. Benny assumed she was returning upstream to the parking area by the dam. The only other car in the lot when he pulled in was a red hatchback. Hers, obviously. They appeared to be the only ones on the river today. He called up to her as she passed.

—Any luck?

He had watched her with the big rainbow. What he had witnessed had nothing to do with luck, nothing to do with the aimless sort of prospecting he had been pursuing. This woman with a Dardevle spoon for an earring did not prospect. She hunted. Her contest with the big rainbow had been the elegant performance of a skilled predator. But his question was the only one he could imagine at the moment, the only one he thought permissible.

—Some, she answered.

—What are they hitting on?

She looked at him as if Benny had asked to peek into her underwear drawer.

—Depends, she said, and moved off along the ridge.

Benny wondered if, after all, he did appear threatening, or merely pathetic, unworthy.

The next week, the red hatchback was there again, and Benny watched for her. He fished downstream from the dam and back up, with no sign of her. He had a few more little trout to his credit, but still none of the big rainbows when he climbed the bank up to the parking lot and found her peeling off her waders and stowing her gear in the back of her car.

—Hello again, Benny said.

—Hello, she said, tentatively, sitting at the open rear of the hatchback, sliding her feet into a pair of running shoes and dropping her waders and wading boots into the back of the car. The red and white lure once again dangled from her ear lobe.

—Didn't see you down there today, Benny said.

—Went upstream today, she said.

—Any luck?

Again Benny felt the hollowness of the question.

—Not bad.

She didn't seem inclined to offer a more detailed report.

Benny thought her an attractive woman, the pony-tail protruding from the back of the ball cap, the peculiar earring signifying the bare skin of her neck. She was younger than him, how much he couldn't guess, but her face was mature, weathered from time spent on rivers. He would have called her neither beautiful nor pretty. If he had been in the habit of using such expressions, he would have described her as handsome. A handsome woman.

She misunderstood Benny's gaze as a call for more information and reluctantly continued.

—A few nice rainbows, she said.

—Me too, Benny said.

He wondered how the young trout he caught compared with her definition of a *nice fish.*

—Took one nice brown, about eighteen inches, she said.

—That beats anything I took, Benny said. I haven't gone up that way in a while. I usually head downstream from the dam here. The water seems richer, but it sounds like I ought to try upstream again.

—It's okay upstream, but you're right. Downstream the fish are bigger, smarter.

—No kidding. I've been coming here for nearly a year and still can't pull up one of those big guys. They just swim right through my legs and laugh at me.

She looked at Benny as if he had soiled something.

—How long have you been fishing here? he asked.

—My second time, she said.

This was the beginning of his second season on this river, still without a *nice fish*, and this woman had nailed one her first time out. Respect and envy mingled in Benny as he stripped off his waders.

She had put up all her equipment except her reel. Walking to a picnic table by the parking area and seating herself, she began to run a cleaning pad along her wet line. Benny stashed his waders and began to break down his tackle, stepping cautiously closer to the table.

—Always surprises me I don't see more people fishing here, he said.

She remained silent, intent on cleaning her line.

—Then again, Benny said, it is pretty tough fishing down there. Tight overhang in a lot a places.

—Not so tough if you pay attention. Think about your casts.

—Yeah, but it can still be a bit twitchy.

—Maybe so. Guess I don't notice that much. I learned to fish in a tight place. Dismal Creek.

—Dismal Creek? I think I was there once. Isn't that up near the prison in Bland County, where they caught those guys trying to escape a few years ago?

Her eyes shot toward him quickly. She wiped the last of her

line, rose from the table, and returned to the red hatchback.

—That's the place, she said.

—I remember it, Benny said. You're right. That is a tight place. Overhang too tight for me. My flies were in the trees all day. She closed the hatchback, stepped around her car, and opened the door.

—If you don't mind me saying something, Benny said. The face she turned to him was cold, suspicious, and Benny recognized that.

—It's nothing really, he said. I just wanted to say how great I think your earring is. Perfect fishing jewelry.

Benny could hear her sigh audibly, and her face softened into a slight smile.

—Thanks, she said. It's so hard for a girl to properly accessorize for fishing these days.

Benny laughed loudly, deeply, honestly. His appreciation of her sense of humor seemed to relax her as she sank into her car and turned the ignition.

She put her car in gear and began to pull out of the parking area but stopped next to Benny, leaning out her open window.

—What are you throwing at those big rainbows down there? she asked.

—Oh, damn near anything, Benny said. Pheasant tails, zug bugs, princes, anything.

—There's your problem.

—What?

—Those big rainbows haven't fed on insects much for a couple of years. They mostly feed on other fish now. Try a Wooly Bugger. Size six or eight.

—That big, really?

—That big.

—Thanks for the advice. I'll try that next week. Maybe I'll see you here then?

—Maybe, she said.

As she drove off, Benny realized that he didn't have any streamers that size in his fly box. He would get some before he returned to the south fork next week in search of the big rainbows and this woman from whom he was slowly learning so much.

The next week arrived, and he could feel the pancakes settling into a sodden lump in his stomach and the extra coffee coursing its way toward his bladder. He paid the green-haired waitress for his breakfast, left the diner, and settled back into his car to complete the drive to the south fork. As he rode the dull, predictable lanes of the interstate, he hoped fervently that the woman would be there again today. A desperate hope. He felt close. Close to the big rainbows. Close to a *nice fish*. Close to that thing at the core. Close to what he knew the woman knew. He carried four huge new Wooly Buggers in his fly box. He was ready. She had to be there. When he turned into the parking area by the dam on the south fork, she sat at the picnic table, tying leader to the end of her fly line.

—Good morning, Benny said.

—Morning, she said, her eyes remaining on her work.

Benny grabbed his gear from the trunk and joined her at the picnic table.

—Back for another go at it? he said.

—Yes, she said.

She executed a flawless nail-knot to join leader and line, a knot that Benny's bumbling fingers would attempt four or five times before producing a bulky facsimile of what she had done so gracefully.

—What's your plan today? Upstream or down? Benny asked.

She glanced briefly toward the river before responding, and Benny worried that his inquiry had been too eager.

—If you don't mind me asking, he said. Not trying to be nosey.

—No. That's fine. I was just thinking about that myself, she said. Doesn't look to be much happening on top. Guess I'll head back downstream.

—Go after those big boys down there again?

—Could be.

—I thought I'd do the same. I took your advice. Brought along some big Wooly Buggers.

Proudly, Benny brought his fly box out of his vest pocket and opened it on the table. The black fluff of the new streamers spilled over the edges.

—Do you think these will do the trick? he asked. Maybe get

some of those big rainbows to pay attention to me?

—Those ought to give you as good a chance as anything, once you get into deeper waters, she said.

—I've got a good feeling. I think today's the day. Even brought my camera, he said, patting a bulge in one of his vest pockets.

Benny feared that he might seem too chatty and annoying, but he couldn't resist, not this close to this woman, the possessor of the unique earring and a wisdom he craved. He had whored himself at the feet of countless fly shop clerks and other fishermen, anyone from whom he might learn something. Mere rectitude would not prevent him from gathering what he could from this woman whose elegant casts could split a close overhang and bring up a huge rainbow.

—By the way, my name's Benny, he said.

—Sandy, she said.

—So, how long have you been doing this, Sandy? he asked.

—About four years, she said.

—Can I ask you how long it took you before you started to get the hang of it? I mean really felt like you knew what you were doing?

—I don't know. Couple of months. It came to me pretty quickly, I guess.

Benny's awe and respect broadened, as he thought of his own struggle to master something that continued to elude him.

—Teach yourself? he asked.

—Pretty much, she said.

—And you said you learned up on Dismal Creek? Did I remember that right?

—Yes.

—Well, I guess if you can fly fish those waters, you can do it anywhere.

—Suppose so.

—Do you live up that way?

—Used to, she said, and stood up from the table.

Benny knew his last question had overstepped the bounds. Too personal. On the river, the subject was fishing and only fishing. He had gone too far.

—I'm going to head on down now, she said, moving down the bank to the stream.

—Good luck, Benny said. I'll hang back a ways. Let you get ahead of me. Maybe see you later downstream.

She nodded and disappeared down the bank.

If etiquette hadn't already demanded that she take the lead downstream, Benny would have insisted she go before him anyway. He wanted her in front of him. He needed her there, to watch her, to observe her. To learn from her.

He fished slowly, carefully, attending to his own drifting nymph while keeping her in view about fifty yards downstream. She stalked the water carefully. Her overhead casts rolled out tight and elegant as before. Her sidearm casts in under the overhanging hemlocks were delicate and accurate. Benny saw her rod arch to a fish at least a half dozen times.

He took a couple of young rainbows, even a respectable twelve-incher, releasing them carefully. His progress was patient, relaxed, secure with her presence ahead of him. When she disappeared around the bend leading to the deeper pool, Benny grew anxious to get her back in sight, but he kept his pace steady. She would not rush recklessly through waters holding good fish. He would fish as she would. When Benny rounded the bend, she had vanished. His stomach tightened. He had lost her. He had to catch up. But at the same time, the morning's extra cup of coffee had finished collecting in his straining bladder. Quickly, he stumbled out of the water, slid his wet waders to his ankles, and pissed profoundly over a mossy rock. Cursing his weakness for coffee, he strapped himself into his waders and hopped back into the stream. Just as he began splashing downstream in pursuit, he glimpsed movement out of the corner of his eye. She sat in the underbrush, high up the bank, several yards upstream from the pool. He hadn't seen her there at all, but she had clearly seen him. Benny made a silent pledge never again to drink more than one cup of coffee on fishing days.

She waved to him, directing him out of the water and up the bank to where she waited.

—Sorry about that, he said as he approached her. I didn't see you here.

—When you got to go, you got to go, she said.

Since she seemed obviously unruffled by his streamside toilet, Benny thought it best to drop the subject.

—Ready to give those big Wooly Buggers a try? she asked.

Her question sounded more like instructions, and Benny sat down beside her.

—Yeah, he said.

—Right down there, right along the seam where the current's flattening out into the pool. See them? Just in under the hemlock branches? Benny knew the spot. He had seen her performance there two weeks before, had failed more than once in that same water himself.

—See? Right along the lane, she said.

Benny stared carefully, adjusting his eyes to the water from this angle. Three big rainbows finned along the skirt of their feeding lane. This was what he had hoped for today. The big ones, the ones called *nice fish*, four or five pounds each, as big around as his upper arm.

—Go ahead, she said. Tie on one of those Wooly Buggers and lay it right along that lane. Right at the edge of the overhang.

—Did you already work the pool? Benny asked.

—No, she said. I've been having a pretty good day, and I had some luck down there a couple weeks ago.

Benny kept his previous voyeurism to himself and listened.

—Looks like they're feeding pretty steady right now, and I think you should have the first run at them today, she said.

Something in her voice made it clear to Benny that her offer was not an act of generosity. It was a test. If she was destined to share these waters with this nosey novice who peed in the open, he would have to prove himself, show himself to be a fisher worth her time, someone worth talking to, someone to fish with.

Benny quivered as he tied on the big Wooly Bugger and slid down the bank to the stream.

—Go in low and slow and kneel behind that rock, she said. Cut your cast tight and lay it down in front of them.

Benny did not speak. He obeyed. He reviewed every move she had made two weeks before and moved into the current. Stripping line from his reel, his gaze locked on the rainbows in their lane, he crept to the middle of the river. He never in his life moved so slowly. The small of his back tensed from the strain of his posture, but he held low as he had been told. Finally, at midstream, he knelt, shot a quick glance up to her, and froze.

—Okay. They're on a rhythm, she said. Start your false casts, get your line out there, and hold until I say when.

Benny began. Breath held deep in his lungs, all his attention on his target, he fed line up the rod and out over the pool. One cast would be all he would get. One chance. It had to hit true.

—Not yet, she said. Hold it. Hold it. Now.

He brought his forward cast to a hard stop, and his line rocketed forward in a tight loop. Just inside the close hemlocks, his line unrolled, and Benny dropped his rod tip. His falling line floated to the surface, and the new Wooly Bugger sank directly into the feeding lane as one of the big rainbows swung in. His breath still held, Benny's throbbing heart slammed against his locked lungs. The big rainbow surged forward to his fly.

—Get ready. Now, she called from the bank.

—Now, Benny thought.

The charge that ran up Benny's arm when the big rainbow struck knocked the stale air from his lungs, and he gasped for new air as he rose from his knees and splashed into the shallower water at the edge of the pool.

—Keep him out of those tree roots.

She shouted to him as she jumped down the bank.

—Hold high and move him.

Benny's quivering arms ached as he held his bowed rod over his head, tilting it, running the huge trout out into deeper, safer waters midstream. He loosened his grip and let the fish run, then clamped down on his line. When the big rainbow jumped, Benny slipped but caught himself and moved up onto the bank.

—Now play him, she said.

Benny ran the big rainbow back and forth through the now-churning water three times before the fish began to tire. Panting, pulling in line and reeling up excess, Benny eased back into the pool as he brought the fish near. Almost close enough now, Benny reached one hand behind his back for his net and felt her hand grasp his and pull it away.

—Allow me, she said, stepping into the stream beside him, her own net in hand.

The huge rainbow still fought. Benny kept working him in, and Sandy took three swipes with the net before she caught him up.

—Damn. Damn, Benny said, looking wide-eyed at the huge trout thrashing in the bulging net.

—Nice fish, Benny, she said. Five pounds easy.

—Damn, he said, still inarticulate.

—You played him beautifully. Nice fish.

Benny heard her. Heard the words he had waited for, the words he craved. He could feel the words resonate in his still-quivering body, his still-pounding heart. *Nice fish.*

She took his camera and photographed him holding his big rainbow. Benny insisted he take one of her holding it, too. His pulse finally began to return to a normal rate as he lowered the huge trout back into the current, held it there a moment, and released it, watching the weary fish dive deep into the roots of the overhanging hemlock.

—Finally. Finally, he said, softly, smiling down into the pool as the surfaced calmed, smiling up into her face.

She nodded and they began to climb the bank, both knowing that to fish any further today would be beside the point, would only muddy what had just occurred. Best to keep this clear and uncluttered for the moment.

They walked the ridge back to their cars in silence. Benny was afraid to speak. Afraid something might burst under the weight of his voice. After leaning their rods against the picnic table and peeling themselves free of their waders, Benny produced two bottles of beer from a cooler in the trunk of his car and offered one to her.

—Thanks, she said, as they settled opposite each other at the table.

—That's it, isn't it? Benny said.

She looked at him and smiled as she sipped her beer.

—That's why we stand in rivers, throwing bits of feather and fur at fish, he said.

She set her beer down and looked across the table at Benny.

—That's it, she said. To stand in a river, to tell a fish a

story, and to get that fish to believe your story.

—Never felt anything like it, he said.

—There is nothing like it, she said.

—Almost as good as sex, Benny said.

He regretted his words the moment he heard them. First he had pissed in front of her and now this. He was hopeless. He would never learn.

—Better, most times, she said, laughing.

Benny stuffed his beer bottle in his mouth, relieved she hadn't taken offense, that his crassness hadn't ruined the day.

—It better be, she said. Fly fishing cost me a marriage, in a way.

—Really? Benny said. It's usually the other way around. The man's always off fishing and the woman gets fed up with it.

—Not like that, she said.

—How so?

She drank from her beer and turned her head, watching the running waters of the south fork of the Cherokee River flowing over the dam.

—Come on. You can't start a story like that and not finish it. No false casts allowed here.

—Fair enough, she said, facing him again. You remember Dismal Creek?

—Yeah. Learning to fish in a tight place.

—Real tight. Well, I started fishing there because my husband was in the prison up there. I'd go fishing after I visited him each week.

Benny's admiration grew with each word she spoke. He sensed he was about to learn something yet more special about her than her unusual jewelry and uncanny skill with a fly rod.

—Is he out now? Benny asked.

—No. He's still in, she said. Just not my husband anymore. Had to divorce him.

She was talking to him now, and Benny waited for more.

—Last week you mentioned the attempted escape there a couple years back.

—Yeah. I remember the newspaper stories about it. They caught the guys at the creek. They...

Benny gasped and sat up straight on his seat.

—Wait a minute, he said. What was it, now? The papers said there was someone else in the clearing by the stream, a fisherman. The convicts tried to hijack the fisherman's car. But he got away. Stranded the convicts. Saw the convicts coming and beat them to the car somehow and...

Benny fell silent. The woman across the table from him became beautiful.

—Your husband was one of those men?

—I was supposed to be the getaway, she said. Waited there for them once a week, all day, same day each week, waiting until they got the chance to make a break. Waited nearly two months. What was I going to do? I fished while I waited. That's how I learned.

—But your husband? The other guy? You just left them there?

Yes. It was a close call. I almost didn't make it.

Benny stared at her, mute and enthralled.

—Had to, she said. I was playing a big brookie there. Must have been fourteen inches. Huge for a brook trout around here. I almost had him when I heard them coming. I realized that by the time they had actually broken out, I was waiting for something else.

She shook her head slowly and chuckled lightly.

—It started out I was fishing and waiting for my husband. By the time he got there, he was just a dangerous man coming between me and a nice fish.

—Amazing, Benny said, his voice a reverent whisper.

—Anyway, wouldn't have been much of a marriage after that, to say the least, so I divorced him. Easiest thing in the world to divorce a man in prison. Now, you probably think I'm the worst bitch who ever lived, right?

—No. No, Benny said, still hardly able to speak.

—Well, that's my story of fly fishing and married life.

—Hell of a story, Benny said.

She drained the last of her beer and stood up. Nearly paralyzed and utterly in love, Benny couldn't take his eyes from her.

—Thanks for the beer, she said. I need to get going.

After she loaded her gear in the red hatchback and climbed in behind the wheel, she leaned her head out the window toward Benny, still motionless in his seat at the picnic table.

—Good fishing today, she said.

—Yeah, Benny said. Maybe I'll see you next week.

She turned the ignition and slid her car into gear.

—Maybe. Should be some good hatches on by then. Start taking some of these trout on top.

—I'll bring you copies of the pictures.

§ § §

Tim Poland *lives and works in the foothills of the Blue Ridge Mountains in southwestern Virginia. His fiction has appeared in The Beloit Fiction Journal, Acorn Whistle, The Georgetown Review, and Wings.*

BLACK COFFEE

by

Judy Pomeranz

It was a typical—make that stereotypical—Greenwich Village bookstore: a little hovel with dark wood shelves lining the walls, floor to ceiling, the top ones accessible only at great peril via a rickety three-step ladder that was shuttled from place to place as the need arose. The shop smelled of old books, despite the fact that the largest part of the inventory was new, and of cigarette smoke, the clientele being generally unconcerned about either fitness or political correctness. There was, of course, a store cat.

The shop was designated, by its owners, a *literary* bookstore, and I guess I'd have to say that's exactly what it was. The owners were a gay couple who both held Ph.D.'s in English from Columbia and stocked the store accordingly. If you asked for the latest P.D. James or Scott Turow, Jerry and Jon would send you politely across town to Barnes and Noble. If you asked for John Grisham or Mary Higgins Clark, they'd turn up their noses, grimace as if a horrid stench had infiltrated the space, and point to the door. Ask for an old edition of *Canterbury Tales* or Schlomoh's new criticism of *Beowulf*, and they'd do anything for you.

I discovered the shop just after I moved to the city two years ago; I used to make a pilgrimage down there at least once a week. I never admitted to Jerry or Jon that I was a lawyer. Somehow I sensed it would depress my currency in their refined world. It's not that I was dishonest about it. In point of fact, they never asked. It didn't seem to matter to them what their customers did outside the store. It probably never occurred to them we did anything other than read.

That was fine with me. I loved masquerading in this Bohemian, intellectual kind of persona. It allowed me to forget the crushingly tedious hours I spent at the office worrying about other people's estates and trusts.

That's the interesting thing about this city, you can pretend to be whomever or whatever you want and no one's the wiser. Reason? Because they're naive? Hardly. It's because no one cares, one way or the other.

Anyway, it was at the Tattered Leaf Book Store that it all began.

I'd read on Jerry and Jon's Web site that they were having George Klingman in to do a reading and sign his new book. Klingman was my favorite author writing in the English language, a man who seemed to share my deepest concerns and one whose books had helped me through some rough times. So of course I told my managing partner that I could not attend a partnership meeting that evening due to pressing family business.

I had read Klingman's new book already—twice—and I brought my copy along for signing. It's the only time I've ever done that. I used to think it was too silly, that autograph seekers were too much like groupies. But in this case, that's exactly what I was. So, I figured, why not?

I was anxious to see what he acted like and what he looked like. His book jackets never had photos, and he shunned publicity. Or maybe the media shunned him for being too erudite, insufficiently mass market. That thought was far more appealing.

But my notion of myself as a member of a terribly select intellectual elite was shattered when I arrived at the Tattered Leaf to find an enormous mass of humanity smashed into the tiny space. Alas, I was not the only New Yorker bright enough to be a Klingman fan. I stood in the back, wedged between a ponytailed early-Marlon Brando kind of guy and an amazingly tall, thin woman who wore a white crop top, hip-hugging jeans and a navel ring that flashed right in my face. Then I heard his voice.

It was silky, deep and smooth, like good cognac. The room fell silent as he began reading from the first chapter of *Orbiting the Mind*. The words I knew so well washed over me, bathing me in their warmth. I'd heard of such things, but I'd never personally been seduced by a voice before.

"*...and so it goes throughout the universe, throughout the cosmos, throughout eternity. Man whirls through it all in his never-ending quest for the ultimate confluence, the* *unattainable quintessence of connection. For in the end, he realizes, nothing else really matters.*"

I was devastated when he stopped reading. I heard Jon's squeaky little voice—which I'd never thought of that way before—announce that Mr. Klingman would now sign copies of his book. The masses began to shift as some people left and others moved up toward the table, now just visible to me, where the author sat signing his opus.

I watched him. He was as smooth as his voice. A big man, just as I'd imagined, blond and brawny. Hairy, it seemed, but I could deal with that as part of the image. Blue eyes. A kind smile. Maybe ever so slightly patronizing.

I was awed. I'm a reasonably good Catholic, but this was better than seeing the Pope on Easter from the piazza in Rome. Slowly, slowly, I made my way closer and closer to George Klingman. Yes, very hairy, but still awesome.

Here's where it started to seem a little surreal. I must have been about ten or fifteen people from the front of the line when, I swear, he looked up and we made eye contact. He grinned at me. At me. Not a general grin for the crowd. A grin at me.

Then he looked back at the books.

When I recovered, I realized, of course, that I had to have imagined the grin.

But then it happened again. After each signature, he'd raise his head and grin at me. Not a cocky grin, not a leering, pick-up grin. A sweet grin. A glad-to-see-you, we've-got-something-in-common grin. A familiar grin.

By the time I made it to the front of the line, I was a wreck. But my legal training has taught me, if nothing else cosmically useful, the fine craft of bullshit...

"Mr. Klingman, I'm so pleased to meet you," I said, handing him my book. "I'd be honored if you'd sign this."

"Of course. And to whom shall I dedicate it?"

"Chelsea Bowen."

He stuck out his right hand. "Pleased to meet you, Chelsea Bowen." He grinned that grin again, and handed me back my book.

"Aren't you going to sign it?"

"I thought maybe I'd sign it after we had a cup of coffee."

"What?"

"I guess my much-vaunted words are not so effective after all," he said. "I'm trying to ask you out for coffee."

"Me?"

"If you're Chelsea Bowen."

I'm ashamed to say that I giggled—yes, giggled—at that point. But I had the presence of mind to say, "sure."

"I'll be done here in a bit. Can you wait?"

Did he know how funny that question was? Did he know how long I would have waited?

So, I strode—and that's not my usual form of ambulation—over to Jerry and Jon to shoot the literary breeze and kill the time. Needless to say, my currency rose immensely, *vis a vis* the two owners, when I casually mentioned why I was hanging around.

Finally, the crowds thinned down to just a few hangers-on from whom George Klingman was clearly hoping to be sprung loose. Jerry and Jon hustled them off, mentioning that Mr. Klingman had another engagement tonight, but thanks for coming.

And off we went. Just like that. Off to Starbuck's. Just like regular people. One *latte* and one decaf of the day. Black.

We sat in tall chairs at a counter that ran along the window overlooking the street. I was new enough to New York that I could still appreciate what a terrifically Manhattan kind of thing this was to do. I felt decidedly cool as I crossed my legs and leaned on the counter.

"I admire your work," I said. "I loved that part you read tonight, about hearts and souls flying through space. The concept rings so true, but I never would have been able to express it myself. To actually hear you read it was amazing."

"It's a living," he shrugged. "How about you? What do you do?" He looked me up and down. "You look to me like a writer."

"I wish."

"What do you mean?"

"I mean I wish I had that kind of creativity," I said.

"What *do* you do?" he asked, stirring his coffee and looking out the window.

"I'm a lawyer," I mumbled, hoping he wouldn't hear.

"Creative enough," he said, "and not *entirely* dishonorable." He grinned that grin again.

"Kind of you to say so."
"Native New Yorker?" he asked.
"No, I've only been here a year. I'm from Virginia."
"You don't sound like it," he said, nodding at a woman who sat down on the other side of him.
"That's because I'm from the northern part," I said.
"Why the move to New York?" He gave me a curious look that implied he actually cared.
"I came to escape my ex-husband who works at my old D.C. law firm."
"Sorry I asked," he said. "You know, you're quite candid."
"And you're actually quite human," I said. "I mean, here we are, having coffee and talking small talk, like kids on a first date. I still can't believe I'm with George Klingman. I've been a huge fan of yours since my college days."
"Okay, so I'm old. Don't rub it in."
Don't rub it in? I couldn't believe he would use such a stale cliche. In fact, his whole manner was somehow inconsistent with my expectations. "You know, you don't sound like your books at all."
"Sorry to disappoint, but I guess I can't maintain the philosopher king veneer twenty-four hours a day," he said with a chuckle.
"Veneer? The person you are when you write is a veneer?"
"Whatever," he said. "I don't want to bore you—or myself—with shop talk. Let's talk about something more interesting, like you."
"No, I'm serious," I said. "What did you mean by 'veneer'?"
"Nothing really," he said, smiling out the window at two passing women. "Just being flip, I guess."
I sipped my decaf, trying to fit 'flip' somewhere into my meticulously constructed image of George Klingman.
I tried another approach. "Tell me what really happens when you sit down to write. I mean, your books reveal such profound insights, kind of commonsensical and other-worldly at the same time. I feel like I'm transported to a new consciousness when I read your work, and I've always wondered what it must be like for you when you write. You must be able to shut everything else out and transcend the banalities the rest of us worry about. Is it like a trance?"
"A trance? Are you kidding?" He laughed. "If I were in a

trance, I wouldn't be able to surf the Net, now would I?"

"Why would you want to?"

"Chat groups. That's where I get my best ideas. Hell, they're like built-in opinion polls. Find out what they're chatting about in Cyberspace and you find out what'll sell."

I felt like I'd been punched in the stomach. "So that's what you care about, what will sell?"

"Of course. This is what I do to pay the rent."

"And your ideas aren't even your own?"

"I wouldn't go that far, counselor. Let's just say my modem's my muse."

I don't know why I so relentlessly pursued the questions, when I didn't want to hear the answers. "So what did you do before the Internet?"

"Browsed a ton of New Age magazines."

"That's it?" I said. "The Internet and New Age magazines?"

"It's no secret."

"I've never heard it."

"I'm rarely asked that directly. God, a *trance*?" He laughed again, loudly. "What were you thinking? You think I'm some kind of psycho lama or something?"

"Hardly," I said sadly. "Why'd you ask me out, anyway?"

"I wanted a cup of coffee?"

"There were dozens of women at that signing. Why me?"

"I liked the way you looked."

"What's that mean?"

"It means you looked like you'd come out with me if I asked."

I tapped my fingers on the counter to release some of the energy I felt building up inside. I suddenly wanted to get out of there.

"So, how do you like New York?" he asked.

Amazingly, he seemed oblivious to my annoyance, so I foolishly decided to give serious conversation another shot. "New York doesn't seem real to me."

"How so?"

"It's too big, too dispersed," I said. "It's not a place. It's a conglomeration of little cells."

"I don't get it. What do you mean?" His quizzical expression confirmed he meant it.

"Oh, come on, you've *written* about this. You've written about how New York is like a stage set, how it's impossible for people to *connect* in the modern urban environment—too many people, too many stimuli, no space. You had all the same concerns I had." I realized my voice was getting louder and higher in pitch.

Klingman gave me a blank stare.

"You've *written* about this," I repeated more quietly, almost begging him to acknowledge it, "maybe not in so many words, but you must know what I mean. You talked about this in *Dancing on the Head of an Idea*."

"God, that was my first book. I hardly remember it. Anyway, how can you say people can't connect? Here we are. We found each other."

"*Found* each other?" I said, then shook my head slowly. "Quite the opposite. I've just *lost* you."

"Could you rewind?" he said. "I think I missed something."

"Don't you see?" I was almost pleading with him. "I had a spectacular George Klingman when I walked into the Tattered Leaf tonight. I had a lIterary voice that had sustained me for years."

"And?"

"And now I have just another New York stage set. Me and some Net surfing guy and a *latte* and a decaf." Without meaning to, I slammed my mug down on the counter. "That's about as pedestrian as it gets. George Klingman's gone forever. Dead."

"Thanks a lot," he said, and stared at me as if I might be deranged.

"It's true," I said. "You're earthy instead of conceptual, you talk in cliches, your ideas are appropriated, and you don't even remember your own books. You're so ... ordinary."

"You don't even know me," he said quietly, looking around to see if anyone was listening.

"So what?"

"So, maybe there's more to me. Maybe there's a side I don't expose to every woman who picks me up."

"Picks you up? *You* picked *me* up!"

"You wanted it," he said. "I could tell."

"God, you're *full* of stupid cliches," I said softly.

"Are you always this nasty, or is this just for me?"

I didn't answer.

"Would you tell me what the hell's going on here?" He seemed more confused than angry. "Why are you being so cruel?"

"Cruel? This is nothing compared to what *you*'ve done to *me*."

"Just by being here and being human, is that it?"

I didn't respond, but I thought that was a fairly good encapsulation. I stared into my empty coffee mug, not wanting to meet his eyes. We were both silent for a moment.

"What can I do?" he finally asked.

"Nothing."

He stood up. "You going to be okay?"

"Of course."

"I don't suppose I should ask you back to my place, huh?" he said, smiling.

I just stared at him, well aware that I was foregoing an opportunity for which, an hour earlier, I would have sacrificed my brother.

"You sure you're okay?" he said.

"Of course I'm okay," I lied.

I sat there at the window, and watched as he walked across the street and down the block. Even from the back, I knew he was grinning at passing women, a glad-to-see-you, we've-got-something-in-common kind of grin. A familiar grin.

§ § §

Judy Pomeranz is an Arlington, Virginia-based freelance writer and art critic. Her fiction has appeared in Santa Barbara Review and The Crescent Review,.

THE NIGHT MARTIN LUTHER KING, JR. WAS SHOT

by

Carolyn Stearns

"Martin Luther King, Jr. has been shot and killed!!"

The music and the dancing stopped at Karamu House, a small theatre in downtown Cleveland, Ohio, as the messenger screamed the news into the rehearsal studio. None of us knew what to say, and so we said nothing. We cried and hugged one another as we slowly put on our street clothes.

One by one the dancers of Karamu's multi-racial dance company silently left the rehearsal studio. I was the last to leave. I turned out the lights and tiptoed mournfully out of the theatre and into the parking lot. For the first time the theatre was truly dark.

I didn't want to go home. I felt safer in the parking lot even though my car had already been broken into and stripped once, the back window had been shot out, and several times the car had been smeared with soap, eggs, tomatoes, dog excrement and other degrading substances. Strangely enough I wasn't afraid. In the city I felt safe.

I turned on the car radio. Many of the stations were already playing Martin Luther King, Jr.'s most famous speeches. Other stations were playing uninterrupted music in his honor. Suddenly, a newscaster interrupted the "I Have a Dream" speech and said everyone should go home and stay there, that an outburst of violence in the city was expected. A soulful version of "We Shall Overcome" followed as I left the parking lot.

I headed straight toward Euclid Avenue, the main artery that would lead me to the suburbs. I stopped at a red light and sat quietly in my blue Oldsmobile Cutlass station wagon, humming sad songs with the radio, waiting for the light to turn green. My leotard and tights were hot and sweaty under my denim coat from class and rehearsal. I turned on my directional light and waited for my turn to turn right.

Click-click. Click-click.

I looked around and noticed a young, good-looking black man waiting on the street corner. He had mahogony skin with no sheen—he almost looked powdered. No meat or greasyAmerican junk food for this black man, I thought. His body was lean and finely tuned. He wore a white, skin tight T-shirt under an open, comfortably worn leather jacket, and a pair of jeans that displayed a proud mound beneath his zipper. I guessed that he was waiting for a bus since the bus stopped at that corner. He looked as if he owned the city. I wondered if he had heard the news.

I couldn't stop staring. The man looked as if he had the power to fly to the moon. His eyes told me his heart knew all there was to know about love. His demeanor reflected a freedom that I only experienced when I danced.

The light turned to green and then back to red again. Instead of turning right, I backed up and jockeyed my car from the right side of my lane to the left—thankfully, there were no cars behind me. I changed my turn signal from right to left.

Click-click. Click-click.

My station wagon hugged the yellow line as I strained to see the man better. I rolled down my car window.

Click-click. Click-click.

The more I stared, the more I knew he had something I wanted, needed, if I were going to survive.

Picture me in my expensive blue box—white-skinned, historically privileged and supposedly free. Picture him standing there, boxless and open—black and historically repressed.

Click-click. Click-click.

Suddenly I knew. I wanted to run away with him—that is, if he would have me. I wanted him to fuck me out of my white skin and send me into oblivion. I wanted to ride him like I rode my Honda 350. I wanted to be as black as he was. He looked brand new—not tired and used the way I felt. He is my savior, I thought. He knows the way!

Without thinking or making a plan, I put my car in park, unlocked the door and got out, leaving the car door open and the keys in the ignition. I didn't care about leaving the car in the middle of a city street, during what could become a crisis. The car will take care of itself, I thought—that is, if I thought anything.

I walked towards the black man. He was too self-absorbed to see me. I wanted to call, "Take me—oh, please take me with you," but I didn't. I was too shy, too afraid he would reject me. I'll go anywhere you want to take me, I thought, it doesn't matter where! Just show me the way! Tell me which bus to take! Save me a seat! Please?

I approached the curb, the black man turned his head in my direction and for a fraction of a second he looked at me with his probing, dark eyes. His gaze was so penetrating that I stopped in my tracks. His eyes up close were deeper and more expressive than I had imagined. However, I could tell there was something about me that frightened him. He remained calm and continued to stand tall as he looked beyond me, over my head, at my car idling in the middle of the street.

"Not to worry," I said nervously, "there's a gas station on the next corner!"

Beep! Beep!

A car horn shouted out into what had become an unusually silent night. My savior stepped away from me.

BEEEEEP!

I looked back over my shoulder and saw a Volkswagen bug behind my car. I should have known. Only Volkswagen bugs beep like that.

Beep! Beep!

"Shut up!" I mumbled. The black man shifted his gaze to the man driving the VW bug.

Out of the corner of my eye I could see the driver of the bug signalling to turn left. He was a heavy set man and his chubby elbow hung out of his window. His left palm periodically slapped the side of his car as his right palm leaned on his horn. I thought later it must have been a tight squeeze for so big a man to fit into such a little car.

BEEEEP! BEEEEP! BEEEEP!

Damn bug. Rude horn! Stupid man!

"Go around me!" I yelled. "Pass the damn car!"

The black man on the street corner turned his back.Clearly, he smelled danger. He walked away from me, toward an approaching bus.

Beeeeeeeeeeeeep!

"Hey lady, move your mother-fuckin' car! We gotta get outa here, gotta get home!"

"I SAID PASS THE DAMN CAR!"

I couldn't hear the hatred in my voice, although I'm sure the black man did.

The bus eased into the bus stop. The sound of its doors opening and closing took my attention away from the VW bug. I watched helplessly as the big blue and white bus swallowed the only person I believed could save me.

"I must be mad," I whispered apologetically, more to myself than anybody else. I dropped the full weight of my head into my hands and a single deep sob exploded into the night air.

Beep! Beep! Beep! Beep! Beep!

I turned and hurried back to my car. As I passed the VW bug, I gave the fat man the finger. Before I got in my car, I looked back to the empty street corner. My dream was gone and with it all feelings of hope.

Beeeeeeeeep! Beeeeeeeeeeep!

I let the tears come as I sat down in my blue seat of respectability. I slammed the door, locked it and jerked the car slightly as I shifted back into drive. I pressed hard on the gas and with a screech of frustration quickly turned right onto Euclid Avenue from the left lane, just as the light turned red. I looked in the rear view window—the bug did not turn. The fat man in the little car didn't make the light. Serves him right! I thought. May he rot in hell!

When I stopped at the next light, I was shaking with grief, despair and confusion. I didn't try to stop the tears—they felt good. They made me feel alive.

"What was I doing, standing there in the middle of the street?" I asked myself. I wiped the dripping sweat from my forehead onto my coatsleeve. What is the matter with me?

My sweat turned cold and my mouth turned dry, the way they do when I'm afraid. I wiped my hands on my coat so they wouldn't slip and slide on the steering wheel.

I hated driving out of the city that night. I was driving back to my own private war zone.

When I arrived home, I hurried wordlessly past my husband and went directly into the bathroom, took off my clothes and stepped into the shower. I wanted to wash away my thoughts of the beautiful black man.

The more I scrubbed, the worse I felt and the whiter I became. I was the queen of clean and I hated my crown, my throne. All the while I kept singing "We shall overcome...." over and over again as my tears mixed with the water pounding down on my neck and shoulders. I didn't see how I could, or ever would.

§ § §

Carolyn Stearns *is a writer and teacher living in Deale, Maryland. She is the author of Where Did All The Water Go? (Tidewater Press) and* ***SPIRIT-WALKING*** (*IM Press).* The latter book is a *Reading Group Choices* selection for 1998, *available at amazon.com or bookzone.com or from 301-587-1202 (Maryland, Virginia, Washington, D.C.)*

BASIC ENGLISH

by

Sally Steenland

Diana Miller drowned a cigarette in her peach yogurt and pitched the half-empty carton into a garbage can by the sink. "Whooa, Miller, we could use you on varsity!" Across the table Sonny Lawson wiped his space for the next lunch shift. "Missed me by an inch but you're better than half the guys on my team."

"Teach my classes and I'll play." She got up to rinse out her coffee mug and caught a glimpse of her face in the paper towel dispenser over the sink. In the curved metal surface she was hazy, almost vanishing. The clock on the wall clicked 10:47; Becky Thompson got up and went to the door. "Well?" Diana said, and dropped back into her chair.

"I thought maybe you were ready to go."

"I'll get there." She lit another cigarette and reached for a magazine. At the end of the table, Bobby Mercer wagged his finger. "No smoking!"

"What's in your shirt pocket?"

"Who put those in there?" He pulled out a pack of Camels and laughed. Teachers burst in the door, carrying trays from the cafeteria. Diana pulled in her chair so they could squeeze past her to the far side of the room, away from the smoke. Bobby slid down and dropped a long white ash on the table. "Why do you bite that poor girl's head off? She's new, just looking for advice."

"Not from me." She smeared an ash into the formica and rubbed her thumb until it disappeared. The clock clicked 10:51.

"MISS MILLER, MISS MILLER. COME TO MR. ROBINSON'S OFFICE."

"Uh oh. Sent to the principal?" Bobby aimed his finger at the intercom. "Act annoyed. Deny it."

"I *am* annoyed. Why don't they leave us alone?"

"Oh, they do. Completely. Terrifyingly."

She slouched toward him on an elbow. "One of my kids fills out deposit slips all period. He pulls out a little notebook and copies all these numbers in ink."

"I've got a thug in Conversational Spanish who carries a locked metal briefcase. Senor Big Man." Bobby took the magazine away from her. "So go, before they lock you up."

She hurried down the hall, following a brown stripe on the floor that marked the fast lane, then turned the corner and stuck her head in her classroom where a handful of students were playing cards, braiding hair, sleeping. "I've got to see Mr. Robinson," she said. Nobody looked up.

Some of her students were chatting by a locker. One of her boys sauntered out of a bathroom. The rest of her fourth-period was probably smoking in the parking lot, or at home watching TV. She pushed through the office door and squeezed past desks and xerox machines to Mr. Robinson's office in the back.

"Miss Miller," he said cheerily, rising from a couch. "Sorry to pull you out of class, but someone here is eager to see you."

A blond young man in a navy blazer stood up and wiped his palms on the front of his trousers. She searched his face for one that she knew, then swallowed and reached to smooth her hair. "Eric Barnes," she said.

"Miss Miller." He sounded nervous and relieved. "I was afraid you wouldn't remember me."

"Junior and senior AP. Give me a minute and I'll remember your thesis." She pressed a finger to her lips. "The Dubliners."

He beamed. "You were the best teacher I ever had."

"Oh yes, Miss Miller's one of our finest," Mr. Robinson said, rocking back and forth on his heels.

"I always wanted to write or visit," Eric said, "just to let you know..."

"But first the news," Mr. Robinson interrupted. "This young man, with a master's degree in literature, has been hired to replace Mr. Ramirez. Eric starts Monday."

"You're going to teach English?" Her hand went to her throat. "Here?"

"That's correct," Mr. Robinson said. "And since Eric is such an admirer, I'd like you to show him the ropes. Introduce him to his colleagues. Show him the supply closet. Help him navigate, so to speak."

They waited for her to say something. "I've got classes straight through this afternoon," she finally managed. "But once you're on board, after that... She checked her watch. "I should be getting back."

Mr. Robinson nodded. "Crestwood's changed," he said to Eric. "Neighborhood's changed. Every day is a challenge, no doubt about that."

Sunday newspapers littered the bed. Diana lay buried with the phone against her ear. "Think it through," Bobby was saying. "You need a plan."

"It doesn't matter, he'll figure it out." She picked blueberries from a frozen muffin. "Becky and her perky chums want me behind bars."

"Since when is being beaten down a crime?" Bobby's voice was urgent. "Let's talk about who the real criminals are."

She closed her eyes, barely listening to his rant. She could see his cramped kitchen, coffee mug and cereal bowl in the drain, newspapers stacked beside the trash can. A wreath of dried red chilies hung from a nail hammered over the sink. "Listen," she said, burrowing under the sheets. "I gotta run."

On Monday morning, she walked into the office ten minutes early. Eric was waiting by the xerox machine, gripping a leather briefcase. Teachers stood by their mail slots, dumping papers into a giant rubber trash can.

"Ready?" she said, walking over. His eyes darted around.

"What if I run out of things to say? What if we just stare at each other?"

She noticed comb marks in his damp yellow hair, like wavy rows in a field of wheat. "It won't happen. You'll get a discussion going and before you know it—the bell."

"You think so?"

She wanted to reach out and cup his face in her palm. Instead, she hugged her mail. "Don't worry. You'll be great." The clock in the office clicked 7:29.

"MONDAY: CHILI DOGS WITH COLE SLAW, FRUIT COCKTAIL. TUESDAY: MACARONI AND CHEESE, LIME JELLO. . ."

In the back row, Darryl flipped on his boom box and heavy rap blasted the room. Two rows over, Wayne snapped on his box and country-western twanged over the rap.

Diana walked down the aisle. "Turn it off," she said. "Both of you."

"Aw Miss Miller, don't be like that." Darryl was sprawled in his seat, twitching to the music. "Redneck tunes give you a troubled stomach."

"At least my guy don't sound like a monkey." Wayne flicked up the volume.

"Who you callin' monkey?"

"Duh, duh, swings through the jungle..." Wayne scratched his armpits and sniffed like a gorilla.

Diana dropped her face to his. "You don't insult people in this room. You don't disrespect them or call them names. Understand?"

"I didn't start it," he mumbled.

"I got witnesses," Darryl yelled. "He called me a monkey, he's gonna pay."

"Not in my homeroom." She sank down at her desk. "Fight it out someplace else. I will not be blasted with music, and I will not be a referee."

"That's right, Miss Miller, you got some jokers in here. No sense, no brains." Sheila Jones sat in the front row, feeding a bottle to her six-week-old baby, who was wrapped tight in a fluffy blue blanket like a wad of laundry. His tiny fists waved frantically, as if he were trying to escape.

"Why'd you bring Clayton in?"

"My mother's got a fever. Some kind of flu. I got a drivers ed test fifth period." She jiggled the bottle and milk dribbled down the baby's chin.

"Maybe the nurse will take him," Diana said. Or I will, she thought. Grab him and make a run for it.

Escape–that was all she wanted. How different from the beginning, when her job had been invigorating, like climbing a hill against a fierce wind. You were scolded if your shades didn't hang exactly even, if your students went to the bathroom without a destination stick. Two days to grade l50 exams. One day to prepare for five new classes. No place to make a phone call. Three minutes to go to the bathroom. Twenty-two minutes for lunch.

She survived each day, exhilarated. The school was ugly, the routine monotonous, the career ladder nil. No matter. She felt like a soldier, a special breed set apart. With her own money she bought books and supplies, posters and videos. She stayed late to plan and think. A lawyer she was dating thought her naïve, said she was planting a garden in concrete.

Over the years, other new teachers gave up. They went on to graduate school and got good jobs; occasionally they called, astonished she was still there. Saint or sucker. They couldn't decide.

The changes were small at first. Fatigue. Lack of appetitie. Next, she had trouble sleeping. Then she couldn't breathe. Sunday afternoons were the worst. By four o'clock she was weeping. One day after school, she went over to Bobby's and curled up on his leather couch. How could she teach AP when she couldn't get out of her chair? How could she teach at all?

He pinched a dead leaf from a jade plant on the window sill. "Listen," he said. "I haven't done a lesson plan in years. Hell, I don't even do field trips any more—too much hassle collecting permission slips, finding a Spanish restaurant that'll take thirty kids. You see anybody going after me?" She rubbed her hand over a purple velvet cushion. Going with the nap was easy. Going against it was hard.

"Why are you knocking yourself out for a jerk like Robinson?" He went into the kitchen and dropped the leaves into the trash. "The guy's a former football coach, for God's sake. He can't even work a computer." She couldn't work a computer either. She couldn't afford graduate school or an entry-level job in another field. She couldn't imagine working through July and August.

Over the summer, she called Mr. Robinson. "I'd like to relinquish my AP classes," she'd said. "I'm ready for a new challenge."

The difference in September was instant and amazing—as if she'd stepped into a different school altogether. No scrutiny from guidance counselors and anxious parents, no flood of college recommendations or field trips to Shakespeare. No inspection at all.

Her Basic English students couldn't find the verb in a sentence. Their reading scores were fourth grade. Nobody wanted them—black and Latino mostly, loud and disrespectful, stupid. "A bunch of losers," she'd joked to Bobby the first week of school. "Instant recognition."

She junked the beat-up grammar texts and told her students to read whatever they wanted. Boys brought in comic books and car magazines; girls read romance and fashion. She never gave tests or a failing grade; any student who put in time deserved to pass.

Becky Thompson sometimes walked with her to the faculty lounge. One day she said, "You used to teach AP?" as if the rumor were too bizarre to be true. "For twelve years," Diana said and hurried ahead. Becky followed, dodging backpacks and elbows. "I was yearbook advisor too," Diana called over her shoulder. "Every spring we went to Stratford. We'd study the plays and take a bus up."

"Really?" Becky hesitated. "I was thinking about taking my class this year."

"Watch out, you're going to get run over." The bell jangled and teachers spilled out the door. Becky squeezed against the wall.

"I've been looking for chaperons to ride along on the bus, make sure nobody wanders out after curfew..." She faltered. "You think you might be interested?"

Diana laughed. "I'll be on vacation."

Becky smiled uncertainly. "Well, me too."

Diana looked at her hesitant, eager face, opened the door wide enough to slip through and said, "Good luck."

The phone kept ringing. Diana squinted at the sun pouring into her bedroom and rolled over to answer.

"Hi, it's Eric. Sorry to bother you on Saturday..."

"Oh no, it's fine." She snapped awake.

"We never did get together during the week." He laughed a little. "And I sure don't have the hang of this job. What about a pep talk before Monday?"

"I think I can do that."

"Well, um... what about tonight?"

She ran a hand down her legs, checking for stubble. "I'll give you some beers and advice," she said. "And a quiz at the end."

She went out and bought red tulips, came home and tossed magazines around the living room. All afternoon she tried on clothes, aiming for an outfit that didn't look deliberate. Finally, she settled on a white shirt that was carefully rumpled, three buttons undone, right to the edge of her tan. She climbed into freshly washed jeans and slipped gold hoops through her ears. Her black hair, still long, fell over her shoulders. In the soft light of her living room, she looked like the old days.

When Eric knocked, she opened the door and let out a laugh. He was dressed like her, in jeans and a rumpled white shirt. His hair was damp still, and he was carrying a six-pack of beer.

"Here you go." He handed over the beer and stuck his hands in his pockets.

"I've got Molson's too," she called from the kitchen.

"Whatever." He wandered to the middle of the room and looked around.

"Come, sit." She perched on the couch and handed him a beer. "So tell me your troubles."

He rubbed his finger over the bottle's rim. "Kids walk in and out, talk over me like I'm not there. I stay up all night doing lesson plans, then all I do is yell. If they're quiet for five minutes, it's this big victory." She touched his hand. After eighteen years, she could control unruly students in minutes; it didn't seem a hard thing to do.

"I want to teach, but don't know how." He scraped his thumb against the label, shredding bits of paper into his lap. "I've done other jobs. Nothing I liked. I'd always end up thinking about when I was most happy—and you know what? It was in high school."

He turned to her. “It was in your class. You got us to talk and think about things. Back then life felt big, like we were breathing the great ideas of the world.” He smiled. “I swear I memorized everything we studied. I saw moors and lakes in my sleep...” He closed his eyes. *Faintly, falling, like the descent of their last end, upon all the living and the dead.*

She swallowed. “The Dead.”

He stretched his arm alongside hers. “Tell me what you know. Please. These kids aren’t the brightest, but I want to teach them something.”

“You haven’t talked with anybody else?”

He shook his head. “You’re the one I want to learn from. I can’t remember what you did, but it was flawless.” He hesitantly touched her arm. She imagined him sitting at the back of her classroom as she read the newspaper like a bank teller on break. He’d see her students playing cards, fixing hair, sleeping. Their murmurs and the rustle of her paper would be the room’s only sound.

“That’s not a good idea.” She pulled her arm away. “What I’m going to say may sound harsh, but you need to hear it. Leave Crestwood. Find a job someplace else.”

“What?”

“It’s a waste of time. These kids you’re trying to teach—they’re losers.” She desperately needed a cigarette or coffee—anything to wipe out the voices whispering, you’re our favorite teacher, the only one who treats us right. She turned to Eric, whose lap was littered with shreds. “Quit now,” she said.

Monday morning, she got to homeroom fifteen minutes late. Across the hall Eric’s face filled Becky’s window. Ten years earlier, he’d been in her room, a lively place spilling with books and posters and maps. The bell rang, and she shut her eyes. Sheila raced in. “Darryl’s gettin’ in a fight!” she cried, “he’s bustin’ up Wayne!”

Diana pulled a tissue from her jeans and wiped her eyes. “That’s his worry, not yours.”

“But he’s got a knife, he’s killing Wayne...”

“Where’s Mr. Robinson?”

“I didn’t see nobody, the crowd’s too big but that knife was shiny big...”

Diana stood up. "Keep the door shut. I'll be back."

A crowd was milling in the hall, sniffing a fight. "Teacher—coming through," she called. "Move back, out of the way." She elbowed her way toward the shouting. When she got to the edge of the crowd, she stopped.

Inside the fight ring, Darryl was banging Wayne's head against a locker. "Punk," he yelled, "red-neck bastard!" A knife flashed inches from Wayne's ear.

She stepped out of the crowd. "Darryl," she said. "Listen to me. I'm going to take this knife before somebody gets hurt."

"I'm gonna whip him til he says sorry," Darryl hissed, and gripped Wayne by the throat. She wrapped her fingers around the knife. "You want to get expelled?" she said quietly. "End up in jail?" His fingers loosened, and she took it. "What are you thinking?" she said. "What is in your head?"

He looked at her and smiled ruefully. "It's an empty place," he said.

Hall guards grabbed the hood of his sweatshirt, pulled Wayne off the floor and dragged them away. Diana turned to the students, craning to see. "It's over," she said. "Go back to class."

In the faculty lounge, Bobby saluted her. "My hero!" he said, raising his mug. "We heard all about it, but tell us again."

Sonny Lawson pulled out a chair. "Teacher of the year," he said. "Hell, let's make her principal."

"Hell, yes." Bobby laughed. "She got an illiterate expelled."

"As for me," Sonny bounced toward the door. "I'm off to the jungle."

"The police want me at the station," Diana said. "There are all these forms."

"Need some company?" Bobby chewed his cuticle.

"No. I'm better off alone."

She knew a complete report would say: "For three years Darryl was a student in my Basic English class. He had regular attendance and brought car magazines to class. He once gave me a leather key chain he'd carved in shop. I do not know if he can read or write."

In the parking lot, the midday sun glinted off windshields and hoods. Cars were parked between white lines in assigned spaces, all of them locked up tight. Eric and Becky's cars were facing each other; their fenders seemed to be touching.

Diana unlocked her door and started the engine. A plastic drugstore key chain banged her knee. The chain from Darryl had been dark calfskin with her initials gracefully carved on one side. She remembered when she'd lost it—running errands one Saturday. Locked out of her car miles from home, she sat on a curb, trailing her fingers through leaves and trash. She finished off her cigarettes, got chilly on the concrete curb. I'll get a cup of coffee, she thought. I'll figure out what to do.

§ § §

Sally Steenland's *stories have appeared in Antietam Review, ARK/angel Review, West Branch, and Metropolitain. She is co-editor of The Magnetic Poetry Book of Poetry and co-author of Kids' Magnetic Poetry Book and Creativity Kit. She lives in Washington, D.C.*

Theodore

by

Bruce L. Wilson

Hmmm. Well, mornings I spend looking through my window at the fishermen on the Flats. I can hardly tell my body from the bed; everything's so watery gray. The attendant passes my open door, pushing a cart that rattles down the hall, and I can hear the phone ringing in the distance at the nurses' station. Someone, bless them, has thoughtfully installed a better eye in my forehead. When I turn to the window again, the fishermen are gone.

As I walk up the dock, I notice the boats are riding low on the November tide. Brown and gold leaves clutter the water, and the hairy algae on the pilings has turned brown. My boat has no gleam in the low sun, and every chip and crack is sharply defined. I step aboard, rocking the tender bottom, and lift the helm footlocker lid to get the keys and open the cabin door. My tackle is heaped messily about the cabin, a reflection of the great fishing which has left me with no time or desire to tidy up. I think about fall, and decide I'm getting used to it.

After cranking the noisy cold engine, I undo the stern lines. I jump on the gunwale, make my way up on the foredeck and take off the bow lines, draping them on the fat dock poles. I engage the gear, spinning the wheel until the wide-beamed boat just clears the big catamaran moored perpendicular to my slip and motor through the rows of docked boats. Boat traffic is mercifully light this late in the year, and the speed limit buoys have been removed from the creek entrance, an annual event which seems to say the water now belongs to the serious few. Revving the big V-8 at the mouth of the creek, I turn for the bay and began to search for diving terns working over bands of surface-feeding striped bass.

The sky is low and leaden, and seagulls sit listlessly on the water, twirling their heads like lazy susans. I cut my engine to drift near a small, sluggishly broaching school. I make a couple of decent casts with no results, then lay the rod on the engine-box with the intention of changing the fly. But I don't seem to be getting to it.

The overblown sky today reminds me of a great fishing trip I made to the Susquehanna Flats with Doc Herr, a Pennsylvania Dutch fisherman who practices dentistry. The Flats is an enormous tidal pool four to seven feet deep.

We were skimming along a weedbed edge, Doc studying his depthfinder as if it were revealing winners at Pimlico racetrack. On the Eastern shore of the Flats sits the state mental hospital, a bleak, jumbled spread of various impregnable-looking brick and slate buildings. I was hoping some of the patients had binoculars, because when the boat stopped, we started catching fish. Nothing makes you look more cool than hooking into a good one, but after several good flurries, the action had slowed, then stopped. Doc stood up tall, looked over the water, cupped his hands to his mouth, and roared, "Come on out, you black and white shitheads!" But the fish remained comatose.

I'd looked up at the mental hospital. A group of patients strolled out front, herded by obvious, civilian clad attendants.

"Say, Doc, I hear the food's good over there."

" Oh yeah?"

"Yeah, I hear they serve soup to nuts."

Why is this memory hitting me today? Maybe I shouldn't go fishing alone. Sure wish I'd listened to Roxie.

Twenty five years ago my girlfriend Roxie and I rented a big colonial house out in what was then the sticks, an area that has now been developed into squares of vinyl-sided tract homes. I was twenty-two. We shared the house with another couple, Rachel and Jeff. Nowadays young people have no qualms about living with their parents until such time as either their lottery tickets or parents cash in. Then, it was the custom for people my age to live in group houses or apartments. There was plenty of room for four people. We had all known each other since high school. I was self employed, framing houses for a custom builder, an occupation I found exciting at the time. I worked hard, and loved the exhilaration of turning a pile of lumber into a tall, multi-planed elegant home. I cherished building the roofs in particular, and felt a divinity on the high beams. My girlfriend Roxie was a few years older than me and worked as a waitress in a nice restaurant in town. She usually worked from six p.m.until closing at two, and there were groups of days when I'd only see her briefly in the morning: all cuddled up next to me and sound asleep, as I rose early to go to work.

We all had jobs we liked; it was a sylvan life. Everybody chipped in with the cleaning and cooking. Rachel and Jeff were both teachers with the county, they were smart and interesting, and we all enjoyed each other's company. Roxie, at twenty-eight, was a mother figure. The three of us considered her very worldly. Roxie pampered me with the plump crab cakes and filet mignons her customers had ordered but not eaten. She was one of those fabulous women who loves to feed men. I was crazy about her, though I never told her that.

The trouble started late one night when Jeff was walking around undressed in his room after a shower. When he snapped his light off to go to bed, he saw a dark face staring through the glass of the second-story window. He claimed later that the peeper didn't get his money's worth, because his balls disappeared instantly. Jeff jumped into jeans and ran down the stairs and out into the night just in time to hear rapid footfalls going away through the dry, crisp, pine needles bottoming the woods. What was truly amazing, however, was that the peeper had carried his own homemade twelve-foot wooden ladder through the woods to check out the bedroom windows. Jeff thought about calling the cops but later decided not to. I didn't hear about all this until I got home from work the next day.

We laughed it off when Jeff recounted the eerie scene. Bizarre stuff was acceptable to us then, we were experiencing so much for the first time that novelty was routine—we were either amazed constantly or hardly at all. Back then we processed events a little differently; I think we were deciding many issues largely upon the amenity of what was the coolest thing to do. Anyway, the ladder got hung on a nearby tree and forgotten. Roxie and Rachel went back to taking showers in the nude.

I was building an especially tricky house at the time with an undermanned crew, working an average sixty hour week, getting to sleep early. Sometimes Roxie would wake me when she got home to make love, but more often than not I slept through the night and would only get to hold her for a few minutes before I headed downstairs to fix breakfast. On Friday and Saturday nights I'd show up at the restaurant bar near closing time and go out with her and her waitress friends for a couple hours of drinking and fun. I asked Roxie if she'd mentioned the peeping episode to the other girls. She said she hadn't because she didn't want them feeling weird at home at night. Roxie was thoughtful like that.

About a week after Jeff's encounter, I got into my pick-up one morning and found a stack of pornographic photos, clipped from magazines, exclusively depicting male homosexual activity, on the seat. Atop the pile was a letter handwritten on blue-lined paper. The note was written in a cursive script of nearly calligraphic quality. In loving detail it described a lengthy view of me taking a shower. Eloquent were the florid, romantic passages descriptive of stirrings the peeper had felt watching me move, unaware of his gaze, around the bathroom. Somehow, the tenor of the note was oddly chaste. The flourishing salutation included my name, which he had evidently gotten from papers in my glove compartment. The letter opened: "Do you have any idea what it's like to be alone, so alone that you must go out at night?" The bizarre postscript read: "Please don't try to hurt me. Why can't you love me? For you must remember that I will *always* love you."

At this point we were still loathe to call the police. There was a contemporary rationalization among us that anyone's personal foible involving sex was no business of The Man's. We didn't let on to each other whether or not we felt a threat of real harm from this pathetic guy. Roxie and Rachel teased me mercilessly about my physical charms. I told them I knew they were only jealous. I couldn't stop thinking about the note, though.

Another couple of weeks passed and we didn't hear from our voyeur. Then one night Rachel was drying her hair in the upstairs bathroom when she saw an eye between the slitted meet of the window curtains. She ran screaming down the stairs, with only a towel around her head, into the den where I sat reading. I looked, confused, up from my book. She was stuttering incoherently, frightened enough to be unaware that she stood naked and dripping in front of me. Then I knew right away what had happened and ran out the side door, into the cold, black night, only to hear the rapid crunch of quickly fading footfalls. Things were getting a little out of hand.

The next day I got out my shotgun and leaned it, unloaded, but with shells in easy reach, next to the kitchen door. I told everybody the next time this guy came around I was going to shoot over his head and scare him off for good. Roxie, probably a little wiser than the rest of us, wanted to call the cops at this point but Jeff and I hooted her down. Rachel said she couldn't make up her mind.

Two days later I got a chance to be a hero. Roxie was just getting in, around two in the morning, when she thought she saw a dark figure dart around a corner from the house while she was unlocking the door. She thumped up the stairs in her waitress outfit, knelt at the bedside, and shouted at me to wake up. The smell of crabcakes and gin on her breath woke me before her urgent words made any sense, but I got the message. I pulled on my pants, ran downstairs, loaded the shotgun, and went out into the cool, starry night. I walked quietly around the house with the gun across my arm, muzzle pointed down. I could hear the prowler walking, using the corners of the house like a squirrel uses the sides of a tree to hide from a hunter. I heard the slight noise of a footfall on pavement and broke into a run, rounding the last corner of the house towards the driveway. In the moonlight I saw a dark figure fleeing. He took off like a deer, piercing the black tree line. I pointed the shotgun in his direction, aimed well over his head, and fired off one barrel, then the other. The bird shot whipped harmlessly through the winter-brittle limbs as the fleeing peeper tore away, evidently immune to the sharp eye-level pine branches. The crackly tramp, tramp, tramp of his feet lessened as his distance increased, fading to a hammering silence. I felt strangely calm. I went back into the house and laid the shotgun, reeking of cordite and cold sweat, on the kitchen table. Everybody was up. I grinned at my three uneasy roomies and said, "That's the last we'll see of him," or something equally laconic.

The next morning I found a dark blue knit stocking cap on the driveway. I turned it inside out and examined it. There was a single crooked black hair clinging to the fabric. That explained the dark face. At least the guy wasn't using commando make-up. But it got real spooky from then on. Two nights later I noticed the the downstairs dining room window screens had been slashed. We called the cops.

Roxie and I talked while we waited for the police. I told her I wasn't thrilled about having to get help from them. I told her I'd appreciate it if she'd let me handle matters when they came.

She sat wearily at the kitchen table. Her good-humored, direct eyes were slightly lidded. She fidgeted with her fingernails as she spoke. "Look, honey," she said, "I'm sick of being scared." I started to say something, but she raised a finger. "Listen to me, will you? There's this slot of time from when you leave in the morning until the sun comes up. I keep waiting for this weirdo to figure your schedule out and come in the house. I *really* need my sleep. I'm turning into a zombie. It's just not right to be scared in your own home. If we can't put a stop to this crazy stuff, I'm going to have to move in somewhere safe until it's all over with." I looked her over carefully.

Less than a year ago we had met at a party held for supporters of a successful local candidate. She had been tending the bar and I had come as the guest of a woman related to the wife of the newly-elected. Roxie, possessed of a charming gabby drawl reflecting her central Texas origin, observed while pouring me a drink, that I had an exceptionally fine posture. The odd, almost-but-not-quite motherly comment caught my interest; we chatted for most of the evening and I picked her up from work the very next night. We spent the night together on our first date as if we had been going together for years. She was the most comfortable girl I had ever met. She had answers to most everything. I knew she was much more talented than I.

So I felt an affront regarding my ability to protect her. "Look Roxie," I said. "In the first place, this guy is definitely not interested in you or Rachel. As far as I'm concerned, I just want the cops here to put your mind at rest. I don't want them staking the place out or using us as a lure to catch him, or any of that stuff. I wish you'd relax a little. I've got things under control. Just let me take care of it."

She looked at me skeptically. "You better think long and hard about what you're gonna do, sweetie pie. My grandma once told me she was content in her old age because she had no regrets. She said it's okay to do stuff you know is wrong. The trick is, just make sure you won't regret it."

Two county troopers arrived, done up in smart uniforms and serious camper hats. One of them had a braided gold loop around his shoulder. They were young, not much older than us, and very professional. After taking a report, they expressed some amazement that we had not called until now. They radioed headquarters and called for a K-9 unit to come out to the house. This was turning into a big production.

I gave them the stocking hat and showed them the heavy ladder. They were very impressed that he had carried his own ladder for at least a quarter of a mile through dense second-growth woods. Outside, I quietly asked one of the troopers what he would do if he encountered a guy doing this stuff at his house. He looked me right in the eye and said, "I'd shoot him."

They scoured the woods with a dog for about an hour. One of the handlers came up and said they had lost the trail at the road several hundred yards from the house. The cops advised us to keep the place tightly locked. They suggested Roxie call me when she left the restaurant so I could patrol the yard before she came in. I downplayed the anxiety everybody felt about the peeper. The trooper said they would patrol the roads around the house whenever they could and to call if we saw him again. I told them things were under control.

Several weeks passed. We'd not been visited, at least that we knew of. Roxie had stopped calling me for patrol when she left work because she knew the lack of sleep was taking a toll on me. So I was sound asleep when she came in and shook me awake.

"Wake up, wake up." she whispered. "He's in the basement."

I came close to telling her she was full of shit and rolling over, but something in her voice forced me up. I got out of bed, naked and skeptical, and headed downstairs to the kitchen. I snatched up the shotgun and loaded it, treading soundlessly across the kitchen floor on bare feet. I opened the basement door and padded down the steps. I took the last two steps slowly and peered into the darkness. I heard a slight rustle of fabric. Every hair on my body stood up. Suddenly, he dashed past me, knocking me down with a sharp elbow or knee, and ran up the outside basement stairs to the yard. I collected myself and began to run. I zig-zagged off of a stored piano and a couple of cardboard boxes as I followed him out the door. He bolted across the driveway, quick as a cat. I took one step onto the pavement and my feet went out from under me on the ice. I came down hard on my back. The shotgun flew out of my hand and discharged as it hit the frozen lawn, shattering the blue night with a roar and sheet of yellow flame. The mocking crunch of his footsteps faded rapidly away again.

I managed to crawl back in the house. Roxie and Jeff got me a robe and helped me upstairs into bed. I lay on my stomach all night, writhing, while Roxie fed me aspirin and rubbed my temples. In the morning, she took me to the emergency room. The doctor gave me some heavy-duty painkillers and told me to stay in bed for at least a week. Things were not turning out so well.

I stayed in bed for two days before I couldn't take it any more. The painkillers worked well enough that I could roam the inside of the house, but the uneven footing in the yard kept me from going out. I called the builder and told him I'd be back in a week. I knew that was what he wanted to hear, but I really didn't think I was going to be able to pull it off. I wasn't getting any sleep, so I decided to stay down in the kitchen and stake out the peeper. He didn't come. I tried to pick a couple of fights with Roxie. She had so much class that she never returned any of the crap I was giving her.

Another week passed and I still couldn't tie my shoes, let alone swing a hammer. I got bored and started drinking during the day. The builder was still being nice, but I knew my absence was costing him money and the day would come when I would either have to return and work badly hurt, or tell him I couldn't finish the job. Rachel and Jeff were solicitous, but I felt a definite oddness with them when I came into a room. Roxie tried to talk to me about relaxing and getting away, but I gave a hundred shitty reasons not to. Then one night the peeper came back.

I was sitting alone in the kitchen drinking bourbon. The light was turned down so low I could hardly read the label on the bottle. I still had a prescription for painkillers, and the combination of them and the alcohol enabled me to sit quietly for hours; and if I only sipped the liquor I could remain alert. I still couldn't stop brooding about the letter though, something about it made me feel kind of wistful. . .no one in my short life had ever fawned over me with such intimacy. Who the hell *was* this guy? Was he showing me something I didn't want to know? Me? Fuck him. . .

A blink of the moonlight coming through the window made me look up. Nothing, I thought. There was only the quiet humming of the refrigerator. I wondered for the umpteenth time if I was queer. Then I heard tiny crisp sounds as someone made their way across the frozen lawn. I slowly rose from my chair, wincing at the pain, and pulling aside the curtain, looked out through a corner of the kitchen door window. There was a short, darkly clad man slowly lifting the ladder from the tree. He held the ladder vertically as he came back towards the house. I reached across the door and grabbed the gun. When he had come in close enough so I could see him well, I turned the deadbolt and threw the door open. He was taken completely by surprise. He tried to run with the ladder, and dropped it. He turned as he dropped the ladder and tripped over it. In the moonlight he was flat on his stomach on the icy blacktop driveway, scrambling to get up and run. I brought the gun to my shoulder and fired over him, at a distance of about twelve feet, but he kept scrambling to get up so I yelled something at him. He didn't respond so I aimed the shotgun at him and fired. The blast spun him around on the ice and he slid slowly down the edge of the driveway until he stopped at the level edge of the lawn. Roxie had come downstairs and was cowering at the kitchen door. She flicked on the outside light.

The peeper was a (small) black boy of about seventeen, wearing an army field jacket, high-topped army boots, and blue jeans. The shot had knocked another blue stocking cap off and the floodlight gleamed from the blood which masked his face. I knelt by him and began to weep as I shouted to Roxie to call the cops.

I found out later his name was Theodore. He had lived with his widowed, drunkenly savage father about a half-mile from us in a little old two-story farmhouse. His dad was a hired hand on the farm. The lieutenant at the county station said they'd been to the house a couple of times before, to check out accusations that his dad was abusing the boy, potshotting his head with punches, that kind of thing, but nothing was proven and that was the end of it. The lieutenant also said Theodore's father had not shown any sorrow when the cops had awakened him to tell him his son had been shot dead while prowling.

The local newspaper headlined the incident for a couple of days, highlighting the racial and sexual angles. I really couldn't talk to anyone about it, and Roxie, Jeff, and Rachel all went to stay with friends and parents until whenever things got back to normal. I lived in the big house alone, drinking all day. The builder understood for another week, then hired someone else. I just couldn't drink enough to sleep. One afternoon I took the shotgun outside and beat it to pieces against a tree until my hands were numb and bleeding. There wasn't sense in any of it. Roxie called me after a couple of days and said she didn't know if she wanted to come back or not. There was something really fucked up between us. After a couple more days she came back to get her clothes and found me sitting in my truck in the freezing cold with my forehead on the wheel, just staring. She called an ambulance.

A kind, dark face hovers over a dazzling white coat: the young resident psychiatrist sits at the edge of my bed in the shimmery glow of the Flats.

We watch the Flats at night. Together we learn revelations are always at hand. The birds, the fish, the fishermen and the dark-faced man all murmur to me about love.

He says: "You know all the things I am saying and probably more. Your reasons are still locked up in your heart. But I can tell from your eyes" (he laughs softly here) *"all* of your eyes, that you're always thinking of him."

The rays from the window bend for me.

Then he asks: "What have you got to lose?" I nod and he cuts me loose with his eyes. *Now I can come and go with the tide. Tenderness flows from the sea-bed and sky; I hear myself whispering for Theo.*

More murmurs. They twine as a choir and breathe: "Listen, listen. You can hear him yourself if you listen."

I listen. I hear the big fish swimming in the Flats. I hear the booming hollowness of their trails. I hear the wind torn by stooping gulls. I hear shrimps clicking rosaries in the pulse of friendly sea-grass. I hear the sly, tinny sulk of sea-nettles, the silvery leaves of victimless alewives sighing in unison, the patient, civic drone of mussel-beds. I hear the seamless wake of venomous rays glissading in review, the helium-grunt of a cormorant stabbing—from a transfixed golden minnow flows a desperate avenue; surely there is too much blood for such a little fish! I hear the footfalls, the crash, the sounds of a blue-black night. The fish and birds, everything turns to shattered bits. Then we start over. Again we start over.

I cry miserably at the thought of him skulking through the woods for a clandestine rendezvous with his forbidden lover, so deeply I ache from thoughts of his thankless efforts to obtain a loving glimpse of us in our private moments—of the boy carrying the ladder through the woods to visit us, to come look at us. I think of his life with his father. The police lieutenant said that Theodore's father had told him that I had done the right thing, that the boy had been one of God's mistakes. Certainly our angels had forsaken us. I needed to tell Theodore that I loved him. I had to let him know what he had done was okay. I needed to let him *look* at me.

So I'm back in my boat and peering around the Bay for anything interesting, it'd would be nice to see leg-long striped bass savaging the darkening surface, but I've gotten mature about fantasies. Soon, I figure it's time to head in and I'm grateful when my engine starts right up at night, even though it always has. I like the way the fast moving shoreline looks deserted in the dusk and I'm glad I've gotten outside of my routine for a while. With a stiff breeze on the bow, the ride back is easy and the red and green light on the nose looks garish but feels balmy. Theodore holds my face in his hands as I slowly power up the creek and back the boat neatly into the slip. Safely moored, I get in the truck, and drive home for dinner.

§ § §

Bruce L. Wilson *of Annapolis, Maryland is the author of the critically acclaimed Little Magothy and Other Stories (IM Press) from which this story was taken. Mr. Wilson won honorable mention in the 1996 ARTSCAPE short story competition.*

Teacher Cog

by

Joshua Wolfe

Standing outside of room 108 in my overpopulated inner-city middle school, I am wondering if I should walk back into my classroom to make sure that I have written the drill correctly on the chalkboard or if I should stay out in the hallway where a swarm of twelve and thirteen year-olds have all ready inundated the school like med-flies on a horse's rear end. The principal asked the staff to enforce the "No Baseball Hats In School" rule, and I feel compelled to respond to his request. I don't feel that I am as much of a disciplinarian as say—Mrs. Jackson, the veteran math teacher whose classroom is across from mine, but I know that getting to the hats first thing in the morning will discourage students from wearing them throughout the school during the day. Honestly, I couldn't care less if Antonio Reed wears his Charlotte Hornets cap to all of his classes, but the administration deems wearing hats "potentially disruptive," and so I go along with the school policy.

A tall eighth grade girl struts by me wearing a brown beret and I tell her to remove it. She ignores me and keeps walking. I don't know her and she is fully aware of this. I am sure that she is thinking, "If tall teacher Mr. what's-his-name doesn't know *my* name, then he can't stop me from wearing this hat." I am thinking the same thing. Once she is three feet past me I raise my voice and say, "Excuse me young lady...," but she has already vanished into the herd of stampeding students. I feel like a fisherman trying to convince a large trout to come back and bite my line. Or more like a traffic cop on a horse trying to wave down a sports car which has just flown by me at 120 mph. There's nothing I can do, so I react the way I always do when there are students watching me unable to control a situation: I pretend that I don't mind, or that I never saw a thing. The contradiction makes me feel cynical, and violated, and stupid, and in the end, slightly helpless. Teacher Bait.

But before I can brood over the fact that some students here really don't really give a hoot what teachers ask them to do, one of my own approaches me and says, "Mr. Wolf, will you tell Michael to give me my creepy crawler back." Creepy crawler? What the hell is a creepy crawler? I pretend that I know what one is and say "Michael—," in that ever-familiar teacher tone of voice, but he reads the potentially dangerous situation before I can get to him and he disappears as well, into the swarm. Melanie, the girl who expected me to retrieve her creepy crawler, looks up at me with dejected eyes, which seem to say, "Mr. Wolf, you're not a good teacher." Teacher Chump.

This makes me think again, at only 8:15 in the morning, how much does school have to do with Teaching and how much has to do with Policing? I'm beginning to think that middle school has changed from a place of learning to a post-modern laboratory experiment. Objective: Train children to sit. Train children to speak. Train children to give back creepy crawlers when they are asked to. And then the bell rings.

Now where I went to school, the 8:20 bell meant something. But here at Dodge City Middle, the 8:20 bell is about as significant as a stop sign in the middle of the Sinai peninsula. It's present, but there's no real need to pay attention to it. It's space dust. It's a busy signal. It has no meaning in the real world. But I decide to rely on memories of my own school days, and so I proceed to allow the small group of students waiting outside my door to enter. "The drill is on the board," I say, as I watch them file in like zombies in a horror movie's dream sequence. "School is surreal" I think to myself.

With five minutes left in third period, I ask the students to close their notebooks. I have an important question to ask. "Why it is important that we learn Spanish, even if we never expect to travel to a foreign country." Michael (the kid who stole Melanie's creepy crawler) raises his hand. I am filled with pride and excitement. I expect to hear a profound explanation about the great percentage of our country's citizens who are native Spanish speakers, and about how it would behoove us to learn this language so that we may function successfully as a progressive and competent country. To my amazement, Michael comes up with an answer which I never thought of:

"Well, you see, if you are standing in line at a drug store and there is a gang of Puerto Ricans standing behind you and they are talking about you, then you can know what they are talking about and if they want to kill you then you can know what they are saying and you can leave before you get hurt."

Hmnnn. "Well...yes Michael, that's one reason, good, can anyone think of another reason." I bite my lower lip and hope that Tyreese can come up with a more insightful answer.

"Well, if you don't know what the answers are on the Spanish test and your parents are going to kick your butt if you don't do well, then you can know Spanish and then you might get the answers right on the test and then your parents will say, 'You did well on the Spanish test,' and then you can do good."

Right. Resolved that these students know only what they can see, I ask the class to get their desks straight so that I can dismiss them for lunch. As they leave, I notice Michael and Walter waiting around until all of the other students have left. They obviously want some "private time" with Mr. Wolf. They approach me and ask what my favorite football team is. Trying to be as sarcastic as possible, I say, "The Pennsylvania Quakers." Walter hits Michael on the arm and says, "See I told you he didn't like the Cowboys." The incident reminds me of something that I heard a professor once say: "From chaos comes order. And from order limitless confusion." Another bell rings and I am grateful that I have fifty minutes to breathe before the next cyclone hits my classroom.

Detention Assignment: Describe exactly what happened when you disrupted Spanish class. Explain how you can avoid these types of situations in the future. Use complete sentences. Your answer must be complete. I suggest you fill one side of a piece of paper. DO NOT WRITE ON THIS SHEET!

I received two replies to this. Both were written on the ditto.

Dear Mr. Wolf,

I am sory that I hit Patricia in class but she started it. She pushed my notebok off of my desk and when I went to pick it up I axidently touched her elbo. She slapped me in my head and nobody slaps me upside my head. You was unfair to me when you punished me and so I got angree. If I was to lissen to you then I wood not have to hit her upside her head. I will not be disrumptive in Spanish class. I will not be disrumptive in Spanish class. I will not be disrumptive in Spanish class. I will not be disrumptive in Spanish class. I will not be disrumptive in Spanish class.

Jason Bates

---

and...

Dear Mr. Wolf,

Jason called me a four letter word and then I asked him to stop it or else. He dropped his notebook on the floor and then blamed me and punched me in the arm and then I slapped him on the head because you wasn't looking. I don't start up with nobody unless they start up with me and so I gave it to him. If he didn't do that then I wouldn't do that. You can listen to the teacher and so you wouldn't get in trouble.

Patricia Holmes

I dismissed Patricia and Jason and told them that I hoped that they learned something from the detention experience. They nodded as respectfully as middle school students can, and then reminded me with looks of boredom that they already knew everything that there was to know and that I was just another part in an overwhelmingly large educational wheel which was a waste of time. Teacher Cog.

As I was walking out to my car, I noticed Michael sitting on the curb outside of school. He saw me and waved. I approached him and asked if he needed a ride home. "No, I'm just waiting for my mom. She had to take my brother to the doctor," he said.

"All right. I'll see you tomorrow." I replied. But before I turned to walk away he called out my name, "Mr. Wolf—."

"Yes?"

"Remember what you told us today about Spanish kids gettin' all dressed up and stuff to go to school?"

"Yes."

"Well my brother always wears nice shoes to school. He never wears sneakers or nuthin'."

"Perhaps your brother has a little Spanish culture in him after all," I said.

"Yeah, that's what I thought. See ya Mr. Wolf."

"See ya Michael."

He waited quietly on the curb for his mom to pick him up and I thought about all of the wonderful ideas that might be sweeping through his head about Spanish kids wearing nice clothes to school. The idea was quite soothing. And before I got into my car I was all ready looking forward to seeing him in school the next day. With a smirk on my face I thought, "Teacher Spark."

§ § §

Joshua Wolf, *a native Baltimoron, has been teaching Spanish for six years. He presently works with seventh and eighth graders at The Park School in Baltimore, Maryland. Josh won an Honorable Mention from the Heekin Foundation for his short story "Omaha," and has also been published in Nostalgia Magazine and The Baltimore Sun. Between Varsity basketball practices and writing lesson plans, Josh writes humor and non-fiction pieces, and leads cultural walking tours in Spain with the woman he loves.*

A segment of life
though short it be
Captures our interest
by revealing
Compelling experiences
as a telling tale

Gerald A. Consalvi
Washington, D.C.

IM Press
P.O. Box 5346
Takoma Park, Maryland 20913-5346
301-587-1202

Autographed and personalized copies of this book can be **ordered** through **IM Press** at the above address. Send a $15 check (includes postage and handling) for each copy **ordered**.

The book can also be **ordered** through amazon.com, or by calling the Book Clearing House 1-800-431-1579.

And for those of you with kids or grandkids, check out the **LITTLE NED STORIES - Book One**, a chapter-picture book for kids 4-8 written by Edward Allan Faine, illustrated by Joan C. Waites.

•Three stories with clear, simple sentences make this charming easy reader an ideal stepping stone to chapter books. The warm, nostalgic illustrations and large bold font appeal to early scholers, while the realistic stories fascinate many a second grader.
•Three seperate stories that describe the experiences of a six-year-old boy in West Virginia in the 1950s.

No Soap — Little Ned and Mr. Jenkins scour the West Virginia countryside in Mr. Jenkins truck looking for the "Man with the Money." They go to the blacksmith, the sawmill, the brickyard, the movie house, and the general store, and (okay, here's a secret) they find the "Man with the Money," but not before Little Ned finds something special: a brand new nickname.

The Boy Who Hated Halloween — Little Ned goes to a Halloween party in a strange town with Caspar the Ghost, Snow White, Pocahontas, Frankenstein and other monsters and gets the sur*prise* of his life!

The Ocean Vacation — Little Ned loves his nightly bath, loves the water, and wants to swin in the ocean, but not with spiders, snakes and goopy, slimy things. Well, boys and girls, and grownups, too, find out how Little Ned — with a little help from Mother and Daddy — overcomes his fear of the big blue endless ocean and learns how to swim.

Order the **LITTLE NED STORIES** as above.